Editor: Paco Asensio

photographs: Roger Casas

editorial coordination: Aurora Cuito

text: Cristina Montes

translation: William Bain

Art director: Mireia Casanovas Soley

graphic design and layout: Emma Termes Parera, Soti Mas-Bagà

Copyright for the international edition:
© H Kliczkowski-Onlybook, S.L
Fundición, 15. Polígono Industrial Santa Ana
28529 Rivas-Vaciamadrid. Madrid
Tel.: +34 916 665 001
Fax: +34 913 012 683
asppan@asppan.com
www.onlybook.com
ISBN: 84-89439-72-9
D.L.: B-4735-02

Editorial project

LOFT Publications
Domènech, 9 2-2
08012 Barcelona. Spain
Tel.: +34 93 218 30 99
Fax: +34 93 237 00 60
e-mail: loft@loftpublications.com
www.loftpublications.com

Loft affirms that it possesses all the necessary rights for the publication of this material and has duly paid all royalties related to the authors' and photographers' rights. Loft also affirms that it has violated no property rights and has respected common law, all authors' rights and all other rights that could be relevant. Finally, Loft affirms that this book contains no obscene nor slanderous material.

Whole or partial reproduction of this book without editors authorization infringes reserved rights; any utilization must be previously requested.

Printed in:
Gráficas Anman. Sabadell, Barcelona. Spain

February 2002

 introduction

 when night falls

 gastronomy

 living night

 nighttime entertainment

introduction

When the sun goes down and electric lighting begins to illuminate the city's spaces, Barcelona is no less bright than in the daytime. Night transforms the day's hurries and worries into a bustling late-hour happiness, wiping away, if only for a few hours, the memory of the hassle of the day.

Darkness doesn't really exist in this welcoming metropolis that never rests and keeps moving to the sometimes frenetic rhythm set by the sea that bathes its feet. But there is also the cadence of the street music, there are the laughs of the night people...

Barcelona is an open city, modern and hospitable, and its nighttime is more than a faithful reflection of this cosmopolitan and welcoming spirit that invades and inspires it. In Barcelona there is room for everything. For everybody.

Nighttime entertainment here is so extensive, varied, and pluralistic that most of the time it's difficult to limit yourself. So much of the time you forget to do half of it! There is little time and much to do, and choosing is the first task for anybody who wishes to discover and be seduced by what the city has to offer.

Activities of all sorts take place in this Mediterranean setting: concerts, dances, spectacles, festivals, fireworks, dinners where the table talk lasts into the morning, interminable pub crawls... there's a place for everything. Barcelona nightlife has changed so much with the passage of time and in such a fast-moving way that places

that seemed untouchable 20 years ago have either closed their doors or simply fallen into total oblivion. Everything passes and nothing remains, as the poet Antonio Machado said. And yet... this is not entirely true: many things have happened, many have died and many new locales have come into being, bringing with them new ways of having fun, new leisure activities, new ways of living the night, of enjoying... But one thing, perhaps the most important, main thing, that is still here, is that spirit of enjoying to the full the nighttime hours, that desire to live the night.

When the daylight goes, Barcelona exudes fun, life, color... The streets fill up with people ready to give free rein to their dreams, their desires, their imagination. They are people who are set on enjoying such a marvelous spectacle of life, of night's fantasy.

The modern comes to the most "in" place, the most vanguardist setting of this city that has made design its flag. Art and culture wearing modernity's most outrageous garb pass through the galleries and rooms of the city, showing off their most diverse forms and languages. Couples walk on the Ramblas, or on the Passeig de Gràcia, seeking a quiet spot for their romantic vigil. The youngest set, in impossible clothing on the cutting edge of fashion, take to the hippest spots to dance to the frenetic rhythms of the latest music. Barcelona's drag queens defy the law of gravity in their platform shoes, lighting up the route with their sophisticated make-up and spectac-

ular dress. The confirmed romantics dance, embraced, to the timeless themes. Lovers of Flamenco music let themselves be seduced by the art of a people whose plaintive bulerías are legendary, remembering in a succession of Flamenco shows the magic of a universal Barcelona like that of Carmen Amaya. Others find their seduction in the rhythms that come from the other side of the Atlantic, and the most daring make it through without sleeping (they'll get their rest in another life) just to keep on dancing until dawn, remembering the night inside some after-hours place...

Everyone has their place in this Barcelona which, as Manuel Vázquez Montalbán has suggested, are many Barcelonas. Everyone lives their life, whatever it is, under the protective mantle of shadows.

Barcelona welcomes them all and explodes jubilantly in a babel of voices when the stars come out... then, at dawn, silence again. Once again the sun, bringing a new day. A day that expectantly longs for the coming of the night to let life go on. In another type of life far from work places, problems, oppression, fatigue, and routine.

A different night but one which, like the night before, will again repeat the ritual of joy, the laughs and the surprise invading the streets.

when night falls

when night falls

The afternoon tones are tremendously attractive in Barcelona. When the sky grows red and the sun starts to go down, the city shows itself to be even more beautiful to the visitor's gaze.

Discovering the most emblematic places in Barcelona at these hours is a pleasant activity for even the most restive spirits, and art lovers will certainly be compensated.

In these early evening hours, the magnificence of the Pedrera, for example, is highlighted when the spotlights of its perimeter show off the suggestive wavy forms which Gaudí's genius conferred on it.

The spectacular architecture of the Hotel Arts and the Mapfre Tower, an open doorway to the sea, an invitation to the city to enjoy this sea which for such a long time has supported Barcelona, and an inheritance of the 1992 Olympic Games, showcase their silhouettes against the colors of the sky in their maximum beauty.

The unique communications tower by Santiago Calatrava rises high up alongside the Palau Sant Jordi and the Olympic Stadium. The sensation of privilege and power is strongest when we contemplate Barcelona at our feet from Mount Tibidabo. Watching the moon appear over the sea and letting yourself be seduced by this indescribably beautiful magical palette becomes truly unique. Walking down the Ramblas to stand before the sea, elbow to elbow with the statue of Columbus, makes the visitor aware of the pleasure of seeing night fall and observing the coming and going of others.

All of these experiences converge into a single experience both for the first-time visitor to Barcelona and the citizen who is used to standing back to watch the wondrous environment from a distance, noticing them, really, only when some friend from abroad calls them to mind. Only at that moment does Barcelona come alive for its long-time inhabitants, as if they had never lived there before.

From this perspective we propose a new way of seeing the city, its best-known monuments, places, and buildings: spaces that change with the coming of night, when artificial lighting from the spotlights and the beacons make sure that no small detail of their beauty is lost. A different air, a new image, although the same but for the change of the eyes that examine them as they are transformed and viewed from this other vantage point.

This route proposes to tour the Barcelona always before us through different eyes, under a different light, with a different feeling.

After years of turning its back on the sea, Barcelona recovered its seafront with the urban reform program carried out in the lead-up to the 1992 Olympic Games. This major transformation allowed the city to take advantage of more than 2.5 miles of beach.

The frenetic activity habitual in the port area contrasts with the agreeable placidity the evening light brings to a space that has seen its physiognomy altered with the city's different town-planning projects.

considered to be the maximum exponent of catalan gothic, the powerful outline of the church of santa maria del mar stands out among the roofs of the ribera district.

The architectural ensemble of the Reials Drassanes (Royal shipyards), dating from 1378, is one of the city's most important works of civil architecture. The buildings have been renovated on various occasions in the long course of its history. At present it houses the Museu Marítim (Maritime Museum).
The space also contains the Café de les Drassanes, an establishment that operates as a bar and an outdoor café. Its doors remain open till three in the morning.

In the foreground, a view of the Pla de la Seu. In the background, the unmistakable form of the Palau Nacional (1929) and the unique white lines of the telecommunications tower built by architect Santiago Calatrava on the occasion of the 1992 Olympic Games.

The Casa Batlló is one of the four residences renovated by Antoni Gaudí for the wealthy Barcelona family. The fragments of polychrome ceramics, the ironwork of the balconies, and the undulated roof—a precursor of the Pedrera—on polished stone from Monjuïc Hill are the most significant elements of a front that shuns straight lines and creates an homage to fantasy and the imagination.

The Casa Milà, known also as the Pedrera, was the last civil work Gaudí planned before dedicating himself to the completion of the church of the Holy Family (Sagrada Família). Its unique whiplash shapes are a synthesis of all the elements that define the easily recognizable Gaudí style.

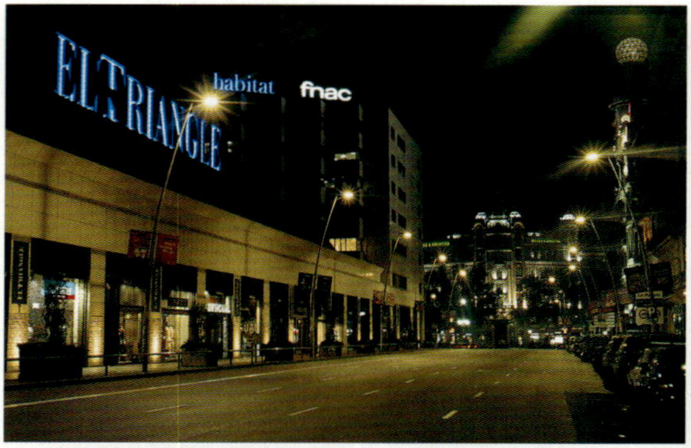
EL TRIANGLE
habitat
fnac

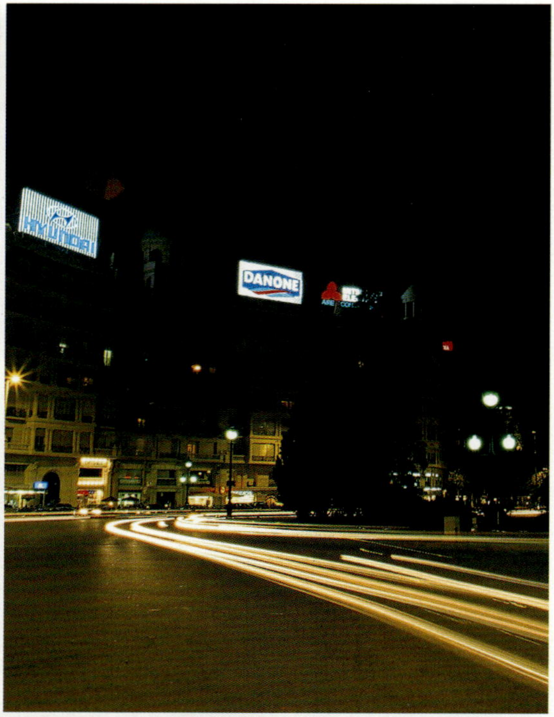
DANONE

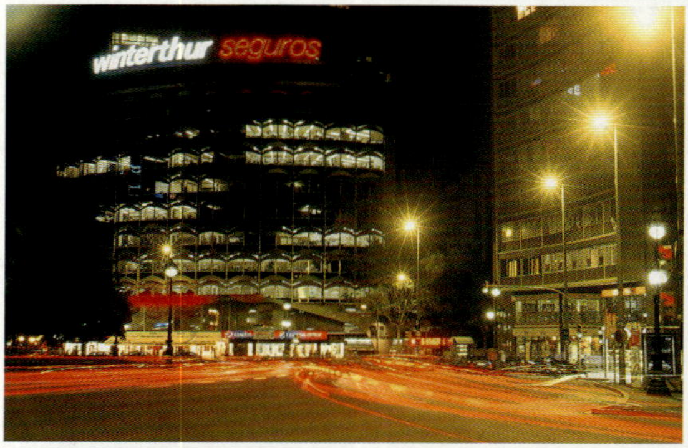
winterthur seguros

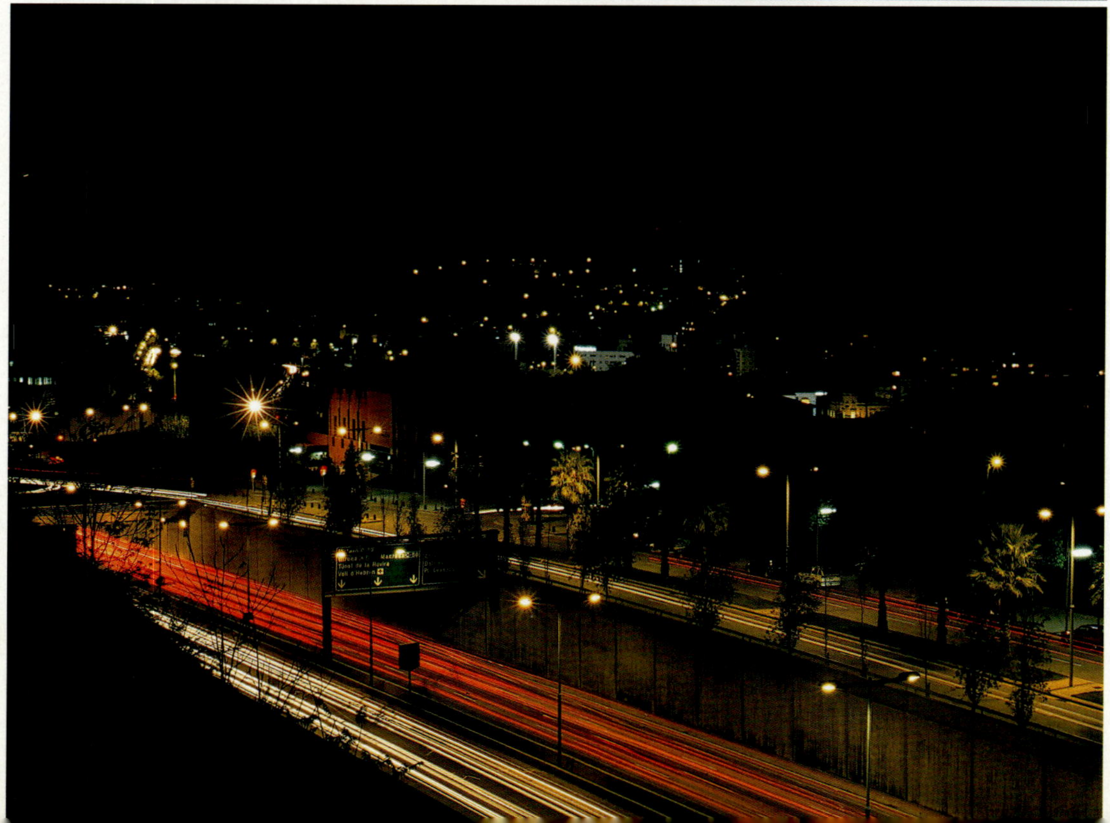

> The urbanistic transformations that Barcelona has undergone in recent years have made it possible to rediscover and newly empower the city's urban spaces and neighborhoods which were in a neglected state. Poble Nou, today's olympic village, and the harbor are some of the areas that have been renovated through the new action plans and conversions undertaken by the city.

famous names in fashion like chanel, armani, carolina herrera, and custo, have opened their doors in the city. aiming to serve a distinguished clientele, these houses, carefully designed and decorated, have come to swell the extensive list of design establishments throughout barcelona.

when night falls 35

As the hospitable and warm city that it is, Barcelona counts on a large number of hotels where visitors can relax and recuperate. The pleasant treatment and the good service they offer make their guests feel more than at home.

when night falls 37

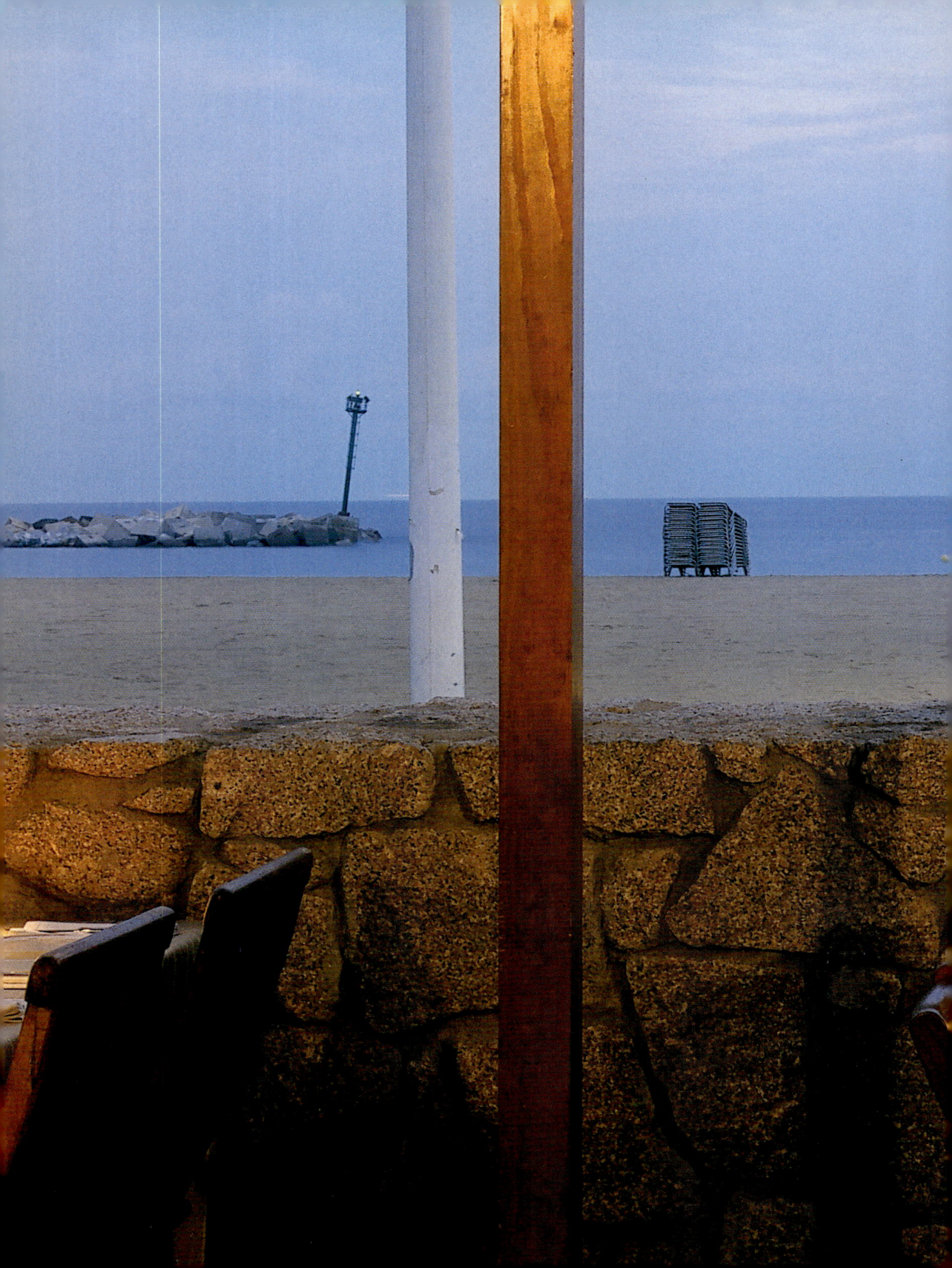

gastronomy

Gastronomy

Barcelona's gastronomic culture can be summed up in one word: variety. All over the city are restaurants that let the gourmet taste the rich and succulent culinary delights on offer. This is an open Barcelona, cosmopolitan, touristic, delicious. The restaurants and other establishments dedicated to these needs are to be found throughout the city, from one end to the other. It is, then, no difficult task to find an appropriate place to enjoy the suggestive food available, no matter what neighborhood you find yourself in.

Barcelonans love to eat well, something which may be seen, in part, from the extensive number of restaurants populating the metropolis. In line with its well-earned fame for hospitable and warm citizenry, the city offers visitors a tasty range of specialties to accommodate all tastes.

Dining in Barcelona is, then, a savory adventure. There is so much to choose from that every palate, however demanding, however sybaritic, will find satisfaction.

One of the main differences for travelers from abroad in comparison with their country of origin is the time at which meals are served here: most likely, while you are in Barcelona you will enjoy something not habitual in your own customs and experience a new concept in time when it comes to food. Approach a restaurant before 8:00 p.m. and you may well find it closed. The ideal hour to sit down at the table is 10:00 p.m., and the dinner is usually a big one, with a first and second course, followed by dessert.

As is the case with the major part of the large cities confronting a touristic demand, Barcelona concentrates its best quality in locales in the restaurant trade in the historical city center. The old nucleus has a wide and varied array of restaurants, tapa bars, grills and other establishments inviting people to come in and taste the most traditional dishes of Catalan cuisine and many other international offerings, many with much more exotic frills. But this is hardly the only area of Barcelona where you will eat well. There also exist numerous establishments farther out that also offer the pleasures of the table.

Barcelona has made gastronomy a complete art where Catalan cuisine itself is blended with that of other countries to make up a suggestive menu of flavors appreciated by the wide range of visitors who come in to enjoy good food. Hence: many things: exotic, economical, creative... It is merely a question of seeking out the place that best adapts to the needs of each particular moment and let yourself be seduced by this fascinating world. It is the explosive conflation of tradition and doing things well at the service of the palate.

catalan cuisine: the taste of the best mediterranean tradition

To help readers chose the establishments that best suit them, the restaurants have been grouped in regard to what they offer: Mediterranean cuisine, traditional Catalan cuisine, and the special cuisine prepared from products bought fresh on a daily basis. Certainly, among these varied styles there exist differences, but they are close enough to make it possible to classify them together under the same denomination.

To speak of Catalan cuisine is no simple matter and to define it perhaps even less simple. We could say that the secrets of Mediterranean cooking are those that best characterize Barcelona's blend of cuisine. This is due, in part at least, to the city's cosmopolitan nature, which makes blending a true amalgamation process when it comes to gastronomic cultures and flavors—not infrequently ones that are alien to this geographical region, but that have nonetheless become a natural part of Catalan cooking.

The cuisine of Barcelona itself, while very simple in terms of ingredients, is very rich in terms of dishes and taste sensations. This is true even to the extent that if one wishes to sample a menu based on Catalan traditions, one must select from numerous options offering the advantages of the justly renowned Mediterranean diet. By definition, it is healthy food, varied and balanced. Every good cook knows that the quality of the ingredients will exalt or ruin a dish, and Barcelona can certainly boast the best ingredients. This is not difficult to see, of course, if one simply passes by any of the many covered markets in the city. Moreover, the condiments count: the olive

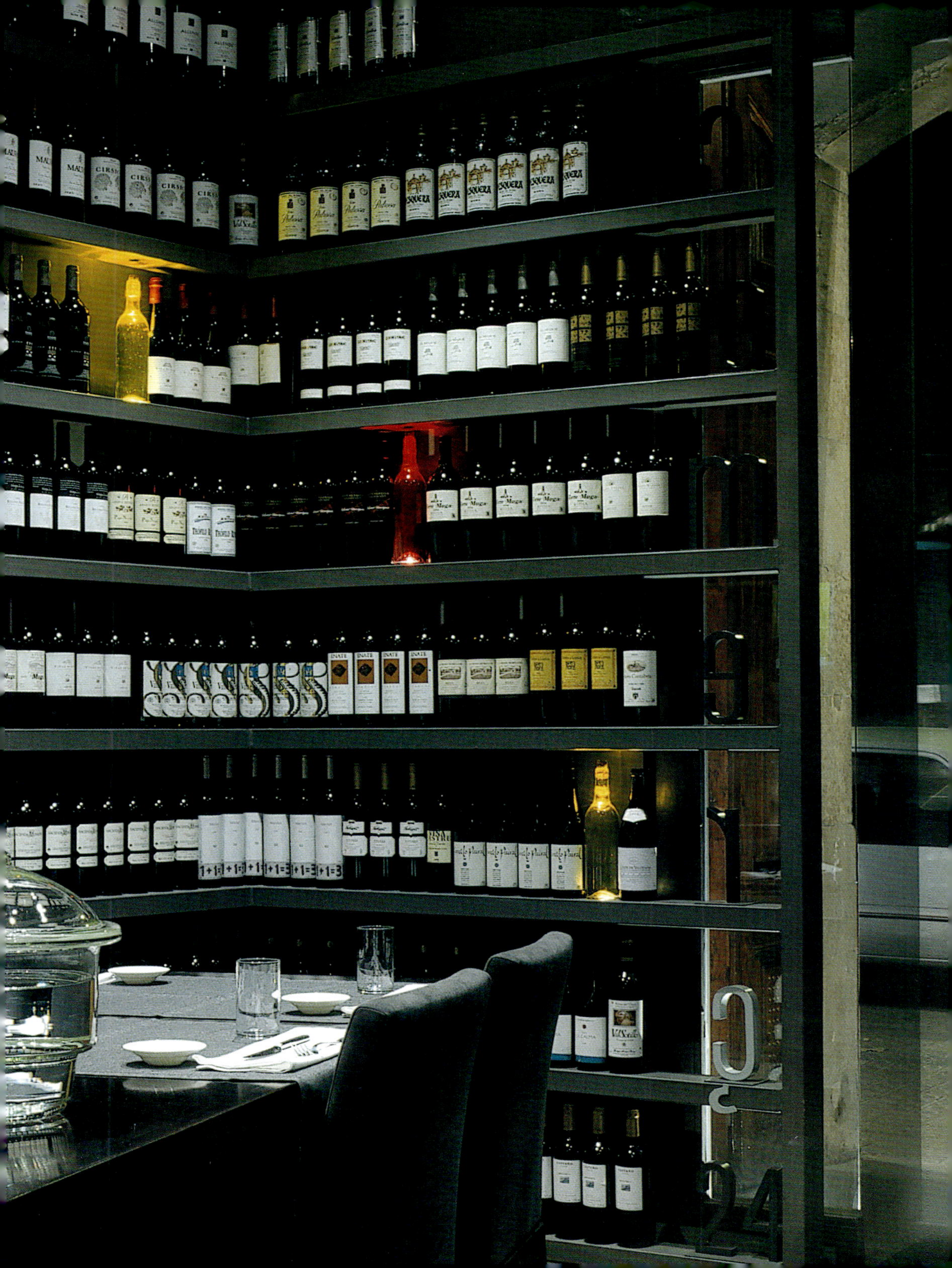
ENATE
Torre Muga
1+1=3

oil, the aromatic herbs, and the dried fruits used adapt the dishes to the different seasons of the year.

On the most typical restaurants' menus there will appear grilled meats, game (a clear example of the vigorous taste of the Catalan country), rice dishes, fish, shellfish. *Escudella*, the typical Catalan soup, *calçots*, a variety of green onion accompanied by *romesco* sauce, or a rich *paella* (most often including shellfish, meat, and vegetables in the rice, and saffron) are some of the best known recipes in Catalan cooking, but certainly not the only ones. *Botifarra amb mongetes* (giant pork sausage with navy beans), *pa amb tomàquet* (bread or toast moistened with fresh tomato), *vedella amb bolets* (beef with mushrooms), or *bacallà amb samfaina* (cod with refried vegetables), and, as dessert, *crema catalana* (a light creme caramel), *mel i mató* (fresh cheese with honey), or *flan* (creme caramel) are some of the traditional dishes that exemplify the most typical flavors in the cuisine.

This type of cooking may be sampled in such emblematic and popular restaurants as the Bilbao, in the heart of the Gràcia neighborhood and with a simple look in terms of decor. It offers excellent meals and has a wine list. Can Culleretas, said to be the oldest restaurant in Barcelona, offers the possibility of enjoying Catalan cooking also, at a slightly higher, but still moderate price. El Senyor Parellada, in a beautiful building in the historical city center dating from the eighteenth century, offers the most classical and popular Catalan cuisine. The mythical Les 7 Portes, at the Pla de Palau in the Porches de Xifré, opened its doors in 1836 and is one of the clas-

The interiors in El principal were carefully created. The result is an exquisite locale where the details take on an even greater importance than they would under other circumstances. Its sophisticated menu of Mediterranean specialties combined with the chef's own creations will convince the unconvinceable.

sics, thanks to its magificent variety of daily fresh food. At the Agut, a space with more than 75 years of history, the job well done in every dish served is highly obvious. Can Lluís offers a family style ambience as well as an excellent quality/price ratio. Ca la Maria, Casa Leopoldo, Benguisat, and Pitarra, where traditional dishes from popular recipes are served, are other interesting options.

In the areas closer to the sea, such as the Barceloneta neighborhood or the Port Olímpic, are a large number of chiringuitos, or fish stands (sometimes the line between stand and restaurant blurs), seafood, and other restaurants. These establishments offer an immense variety of sea products, from small fry to large, rice dishes, and tapas. If you are new to Mediterranean food, you will be pleasantly surprised. A must is Can Costa, on Barceloneta beach, which offers traditional rice dishes, pasta dishes, shellfish dishes, and fish; the Passadís d'el Pep, good seafood made from the best daily fresh products; or Cal Pinxo, a restaurant that continues to prepare traditional *tasca* (tavern, in an older sense) cooking even though most of the beach stands that once filled Barceloneta have disappeared. Still another option, quite close to this area, is to visit the Agua Restaurant, where the same seafood and general Mediterranean cuisine may be enjoyed while contemplating the marvelous spectacle offered by the sea itself.

Because of the geographical proximity and certain similarities regarding the preparation of certain dishes, you

The Mediterranean is on all four sides, making the major protagonist in Agua the sea, both by way of its placement on the beach and by way of the cooking style on offer. Fresh, informal, nautical decoration—de rigueur in a place seeking to delight you with the most succulent recipes from the sea of seas—also includes a light touch of modernity.

shouldn't leave out the typical gastronomy of other parts of Spain, also present on the menu in many Barcelonan restaurants to allow the traveler to appreciate the specialties of other areas of the country.

Basque cuisine, for example, is well represented at the Maitetxu; the Táktika Berri, which was formerly a soccer club; the Gorria, whose professional rigor defines its offer; or the Font de Llúria, specialists in the Vasco-Navarra region.

The Hostal El Pintor will delight you with exquisite Andalusian tastes, and the Furacu presents Asturia's delicious cuisine.

Galician cooking finds its strongest expression at the Casa Darío, an establishment that has put in more than 30 years of offering the best cuisine from Galicia in Barcelona; in Rías de Galicia, Santiaguiño, Mesón Morriña or Medulio, and in a numerous other fish restaurants you will find the same specialty.

Lovers of Castilian style food will want to try Asador de Aranda, a classic uptown establishment offering this specialty; Hermanos Tomás has an attractive variety of products from Castile, and there is also Asador de Burgos, whose offering always includes a good cellar. The list of establishments offering specialties of Catalan cuisine, as well as gastronomic dishes from the other regions of Spain would prove interminable.

comerç 24 is a design restaurant on the cutting edge that brings the client savory dishes and imaginative tapas. The cuisine is prepared from daily fresh ingredients and is simple and subtle, the products used carefully selected from the day's array in the centrally located Boqueria Market.

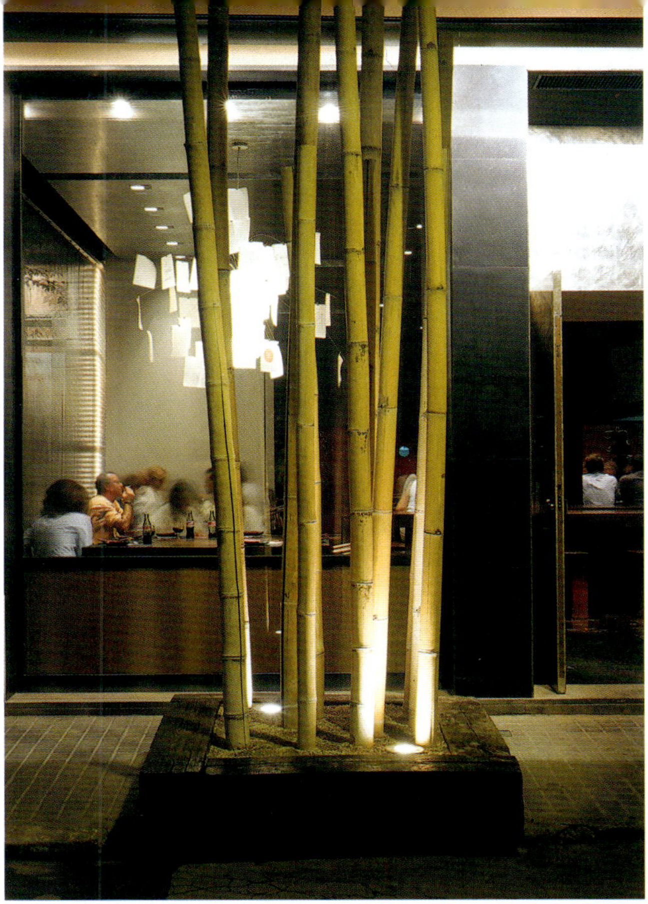

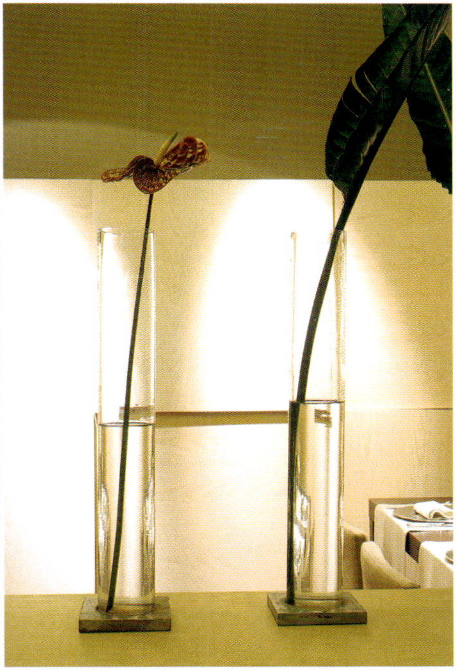

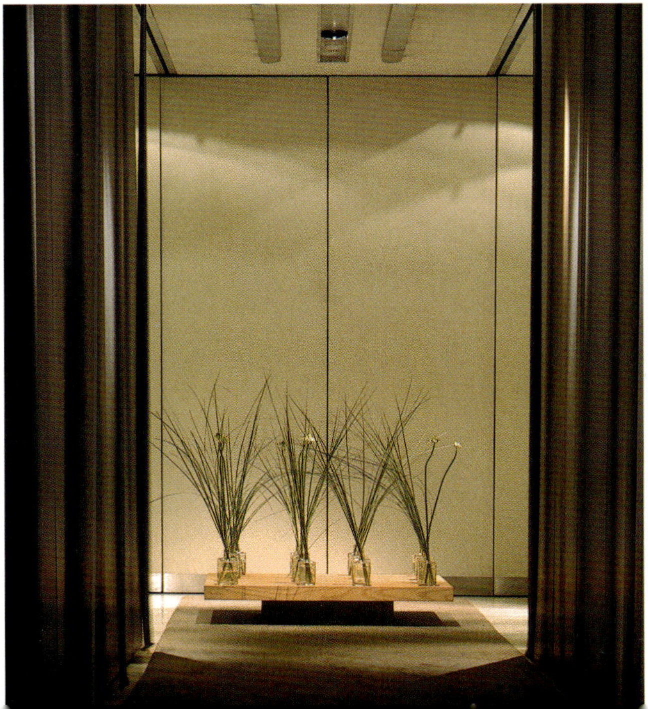

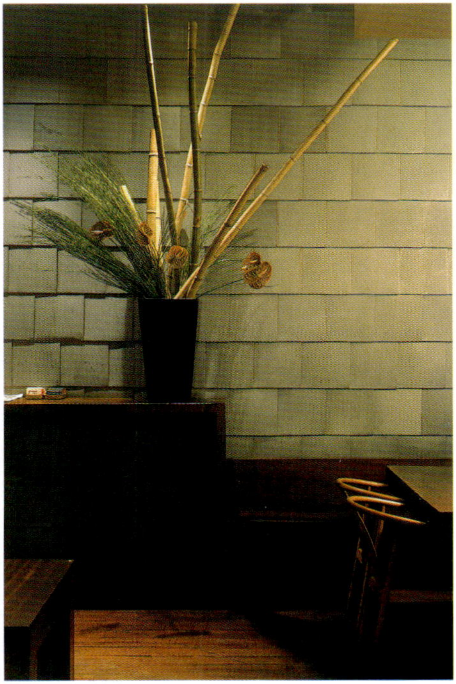

around the world's cuisines

Trying specialties from other countries, discovering the *delicatessens* of exotic places, or succumbing to the caprices of French, for example, or Mexican cooking is also possible in Barcelona, a city that has, as you may want to do, let itself be seduced by the flavors and sensations of other cultures. And it shows this generously in many of the restaurants that are distributed throughout its area from sea to mountain. Establishments with Egyptian proposals, Lebanese, Indian, Pakistani, for example, or Indonesian, or Cuban.... They proliferate and seduce through their exquisite favorite spices and textures. This does not mean, of course, that European cuisine, with French and Italian chefs heading the list, in any way loses out in the competition.

As if it were a question of an enormous table covered with specialties, the Asiatic continent is present with an endless culinary offer where rice, exotic fruits, spices, and fish are the starring ingredients. Specialties from **India**, a rich and extensive region whose cooking is filled with the same variety that exists in its culture (spices, herbs, seeds, among the basic ingredients) may be sampled at such places as the Govinda or the Alchalal.

The unique dishes in **Thai** food, another cuisine that has been in increased demand in the West in recent years, contains different varieties of lime, different kinds of basil, vegetables or dried shrimp...; one of the restaurants that offers the best of this specialty is Thaï Gardens. **Korean** cuisine, marked by the great influence of Chinese and Japanese cooking, has its own simple character, delicate and particular. Soups, fish dishes, and vegetables

Japanese cuisine, with a fast growing number of enthusiasts, is well represented in locales like El Japonés and Taira. Both are restaurants of minimalist aesthetic, sober and sophisticated, in keeping with the cuisine they serve. Also, both will permit lovers of Nipponese specialties to satisfy their subtlest gastronomic desires.

are among the main ingredients in Korean, as in many Asiatic cuisines, and it has five essential tastes: sour, sweet, salty, piquant, and bitter, present in soy sauce, ginseng, pepper, rice wine, or cherry wine, for example. The Shila and the Han In Jong have all of these.

China is another of these places with a long tradition of tastes. Barcelona has many restaurants that offer Chinese cuisine. Two of the best are the Río Azul and the Pekín. A third good choice here would be the Wok & Bol, a family restaurant that is the result of a meeting of the Catalan and the Chinese, with no loss to either.

Japanese gastronomy is based on the art of the simple, and it is an exquisite, delicate food much appreciated the world over. This culture begins with the concept that eating is a feast for the palate and for the spirit, a ritual that you may want to live in the Yashima or in the Sushi, a locale that goes back more than 20 years, and in the Shojiro and the Satoru Miyano.

If Asiatic cooking and taste diversity in all its variety of culinary styles pleases you, Arabic cuisine also has a great complexity of flavors and aromas, carefully prepared according to given dietary rules in the Islamic religion (among them, fasting and the prohibition against eating pork products). In this style of cooking there is also a predilection for vegetables and milk products. Arabic cuisine is to be found in Al Diwan, for example, where it is possible enjoy authentic **Lebanese** food, or the Syndbad, the Karakala, or the Abou-Khalil. Other specialties,

Il Giardinetto is the ideal place for those who wish to enjoy the delights of traditional Italian cuisine: the à la carte service is excellent. Il Giardinetto is an establishment that has been very carefully laid out, and it breathes an ambience of things intellectual, sophisticated, romantic and intimist.

The extensive gastronomic array offered visitors in the city of Barcelona at the dinner hour doesn't make choosing an easy matter.
Barcelonans love to eat, and this is seen in the fact that all of the culinary varieties cited here are represented in the Catalan capital.

EL J
APO
NÉS

such as **Moroccan**, are offered at La Rosa del Desierto, the pioneer in these delicious tastes in Barcelona. **Israeli** restaurants also offer their special fare in, for example, the Babilònia, and the Mesopotamia, offers rich exotic dishes made from **Iraqui** recipes and southern Turkey. Traditional **Turkish** dishes are also available at La Luna de Estambul.

Typical food from South American countries is also represented in Barcelona: the traditional Argentinian asados, spicy Mexican, Cuban, Peruvian, or Brazilian specialties... Los Años Locos is ideal for tasting pure **Argentinian** cuisine, as is Los Asadores. El Tanguito, in the heart of the Eixample Quarter, or Las Cuartetas, are two other good locales if you wish to discover the taste sensations of a country with a great gastronomic richness. **Mexican** cuisine can also be sampled in Margarita Blue, a place that is also an elegant bar and whose specialty is mestiza (mixed) and informal dishes, a touch they call "mexditerráneo." Places like La Cantina, Ay Caramba or México Lindo serve authentic Mexican cuisine. The tasty **Cuban** style is to be found in Habana Barcelona; dishes typical of **Uruguay** in La Rueda or La Carreta. **Brazil's** secrets are in Chimarrao, and those of **Columbia** in El Celler de Macondo or in Restaurante La Flaca..

From France to Bulgaria passing through Greece and Italy, European cuisine finds numerous establishments to represent it in Barcelona. The well-deserved fame of **French** chefs is too well known to need much rehearsal here.

Barcelona is among those cities where the design concept goes beyond the superficial. Not by chance do there exist guidebooks calling attention to these establishments purely because of their aesthetics. The majority of these places have, it is true, taken pains with their decor, and they have achieved attractive spaces, suggestive and full of personality, catering to a clientele which, besides knowing how to enjoy the cuisine, is also able to appreciate the environment.

French food is certainly a reality in Barcelona, and in its gastronomy there coexist endless varieties of tastes which without the least doubt are not unfamiliar here, given the geographical proximity with Barcelona. The virtues of this cuisine can be appreciated in La Camarga, which offers specialties from the south of France; La Maison du Languedoc Rousillon; Le Café Bristot; or Le Petit Bergerac.

And if the French tradition is famed for its exquisiteness and delicacy, the **Italian** is distinguished by the variety of tastes from its regions: Tuscany has a simple cuisine based on pasta, bread, fruits, vegetables, and cheese. Sicilian fare is influenced by the Arabic, hence the blend of sweet and salty tastes. In Venice, the cuisine shows notable exotic touches, and in Rome it is possible to discover flavors that originated with the Etruscans. The legacy of the ancient Roman Empire has placed no restrictions on appetite, aromas or tastes. The Little Italy Restaurant or Da Paolo are a luxury for the most Epicurean palates. Il Bellini proposes discovery of the authentic Italian cuisine; Lungomare is a locale that deserves to pride itself on offering quality, innovation and creativity.

Greek, with ample diversity of basic yogurt dishes, can be enjoyed in restaurants like Dionisos, La Taberna de Oriente, or Planet Greece.

other ways of dining

One of the ways the Spanish fill their stomachs is the **tapa**. You know that Barcelona would not, then, forget about this gastronomic species. Tapas were born during the Middle Ages in order to avoid drinking wine on an empty stomach. A royal decree obliged innkeepers to serve jugs of wine with a small plate atop it by way of covering (tapa) and on this cover a small ration of food was served. Thus the birth of the tapa, which, with the passage of time, has become a unique way of satisfying one's appetite standing at a bar among friends and potential friends. There are tapa areas of in the city, with the neighborhoods of Gràcia, Ciutat Vella, and Born being the most adept in this art: consider, for example, the Bodega Sepúlveda, Cervesería Catalana, or Euskal Etxea, this last-named place a pioneer in the Basque tapa boom. Also not to be missed is Quimet & Quimet, Irati, and Santa Maria.

For those who prefer **specialized restaurants**, Flash-Flash, one of the most emblematic in the city, earned its fame over the course of more than 30 years and has remained above all stylistic changes. Fondue lovers should not forget to stop by La Carassa, a unique locale offering an extensive assortment of this specialty. And all of those who simply can't resist mussels have a date with La Muscleria, an idea imported from Belgium and offering more than 30 different varieties. Chicken lovers will want to visit the Central Catalana del Pollastre, and those who live by cheese alone won't be able to leave the city without visiting Tutusaus, a paradise for the most elitist palates.

omelet enthusiasts will want to try flash-flash, an emblematic locale born in the 1970s; those enamoured of one-of tapas should visit the santa maria, where haute cuisine comes right out onto the street to be with everybody.

For those who somehow miss the dinner hour, there's no need to worry as there are establishments that serve meals **until midnight**. Late meals are served past the witching hour at No me Quite Pá, Les Bruixes, the Restaurant del TNC, El Salero or El Chiringuito Escribá.

Other suggestions are **fast-food** chains (not a good choice for the gourmet, but appropriate if used in emergency). The internationally known McDonald's, Burger King, Kentucky Fried Chicken, and Pizza Hut share the Barcelona streets with other chains like Boccata or Pans & Company.

For those in search of **design cuisine**, as it were, those who enjoy tasting unique combinations and new dishes, there are other locales in Barcelona. Masters of the cut of Carles Gaig, Juan Badía, or Felip Planas and Oriol Laguer, trained in the school of Ferran Adrià have exquisite spaces where the most innovative recipes are served: Ot, Molina Charcutería, Pou Dolç, Estrella de Plata or Tram-Tram offer the latest secrets of the great. Other locales for the most sybaritic and refined palates are Talaia Mar, Merlot, Neichel, Escola de Restauració, Jaume de Provença or Gaig.

Definitively, a grand assortment allowing travelers to choose what best suits them at any given moment of the day or night.

graphic design

Graphic design is an added value for things culinary in Barcelona's restaurants. Proposals multiply when it comes to designing images, and the creative imagination is boundless.

SANTA MARIA
BARCELONA IBIZA

NEGRO **PRINCIPAL** MORDISCO
TRAGAMAR ELJ APO NÉS
ACONTRALUZ
MORDISCO EN CASA
TRAGALUZ AGUA
TRAGALUZ EN CASA

GRUPO TRAGALUZ
T 93 487 76 72   F 93 216 07 50
Passeig de Gracia 60 2°B
08007 Barcelona
www.grupotragaluz.com

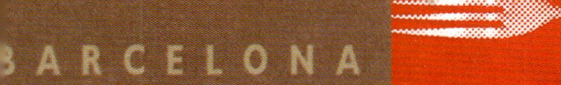

ELJ APO NÉS

日 本 語

NEGRO

FLASH FLASH
tortillería
La Granada del Penedès, 25 - 08006 Barcelona
Tel 93 237 09 90 - Fax 93 415 98 56

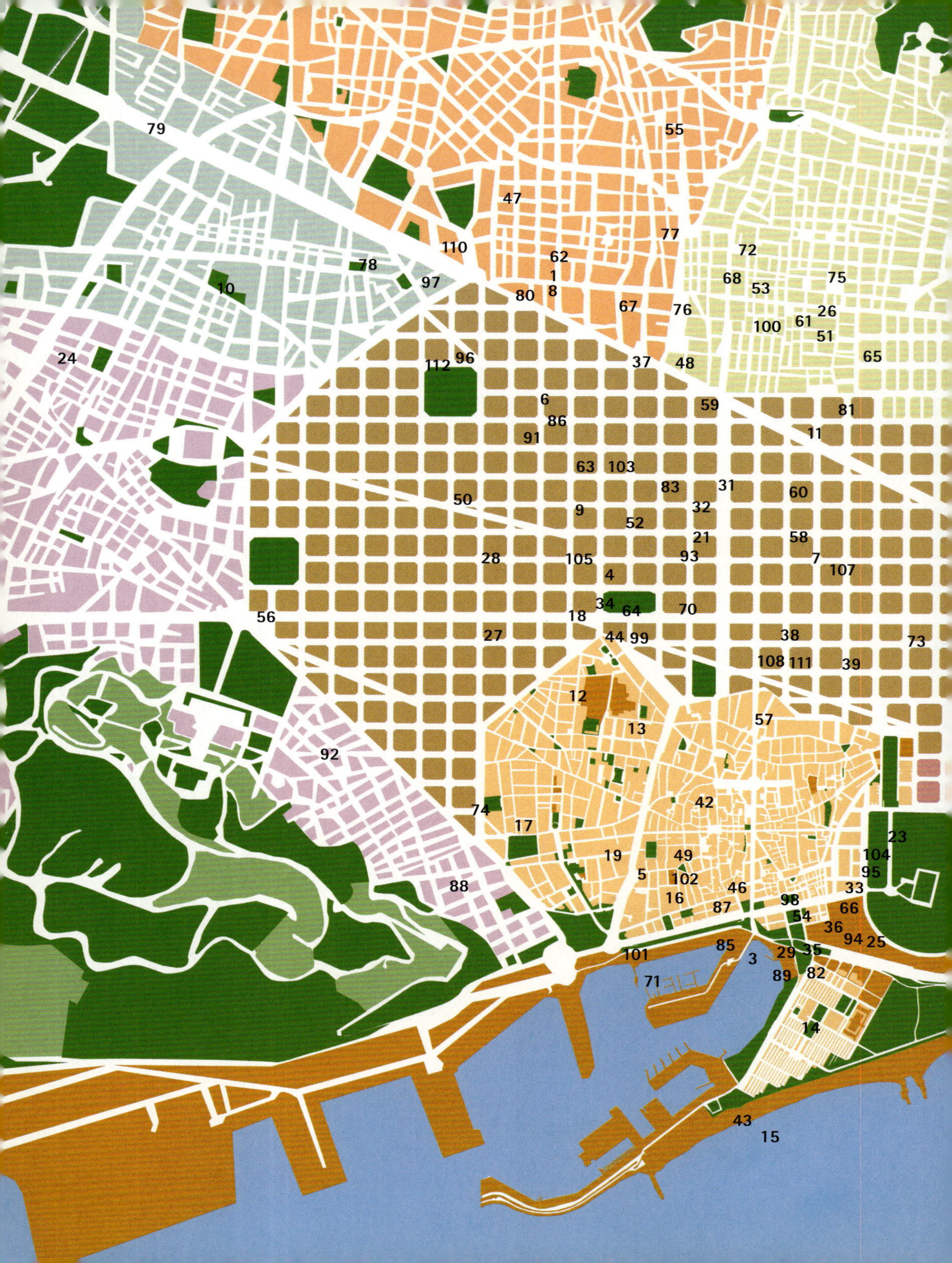
79
55
47
77
110
62
72
78
1
68
53
75
97
10
80
8
67
76
26
61
100
51
24
96
112
37
48
65
6
59
81
86
91
11
63
103
83
31
60
50
9
52
32
21
58
28
105
93
7
107
4
34
64
70
56
18
44
99
27
38
73
108
111
39
12
13
57
92
42
74
17
23
104
19
49
5
102
95
88
46
33
16
98
87
66
54
36
94
25
85
101
29
35
3
89
82
71
14
43
15

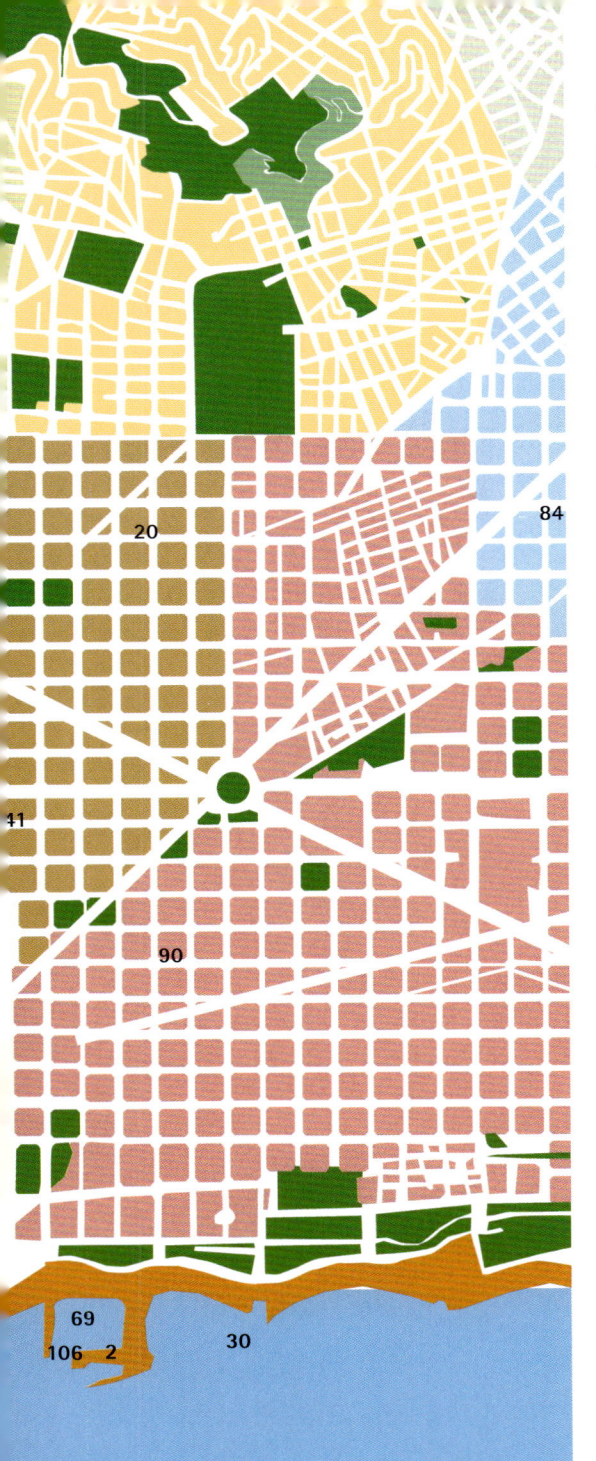

gastronomy: practical information

1. ABOU-KHALIL. Santaló, 88 ☎ 932 018 830
2. AGUA. Passeig Marítim, 30 ☎ 932 251 272
3. AGUT. Gignàs, 16 ☎ 933 151 709
4. AL DIWAN. València, 218 ☎ 934 540 712
5. ALCHALAL. L'Arc de Sant Agustí, 5 ☎ 933 013 467
6. ASADOR DE ARANDA. Londres, 94 ☎ 934 146 790
7. ASADOR DE BURGOS. Bruc, 118 ☎ 932 073 160
8. AY, CARAMBA. Santaló, 85 ☎ 932 004 190
9. BABILÒNIA. Provença, 202 ☎ 934 548 869
10. BENGUISAT. Déu i Mata, 12 ☎ 934 050 242
11. BILBAO. Perill, 33 ☎ 934 571 390
12. BODEGA SEPÚLVEDA. Sepúlveda, 173 bis ☎ 934 547 094
13. CA LA MARIA. Tallers, 76 bis ☎ 933 188 993
14. CAL PINXO. Plaça Pau Vila, 1 ☎ 932 212 211
15. CAN COSTA. Passeig Joan de Borbó, 70 ☎ 932 219 511
16. CAN CULLERETES. Quintana, 5 ☎ 933 173 022
17. CAN LLUÍS. Cera, 49 ☎ 934 411 187
18. CASA DARÍO. Consell de Cent, 256 ☎ 934 533 135
19. CASA LEOPOLDO. Sant Rafael, 24 ☎ 934 413 014
20. CENTRAL CATALANA DEL POLLASTRE. Padilla, 323 ☎ 934 360 010
21. CERVESERIA CATALANA. Mallorca, 236 ☎ 932 160 368
22. CHIMARRAO. Metal·lúrgia, 100 ☎ 932 230 793 (not on map)
23. COMERÇ 24. Comerç, 24 ☎ 933 192 102
24. DA PAOLO. Avinguda Madrid, 63-73 ☎ 934 904 891
25. DIONISOS. Avinguda Marquès de l'Argentera, 27 ☎ 932 682 472
26. DIONISOS. Torrent de l'Olla, 144 ☎ 932 373 417
27. DIONISOS. Urgell, 90 ☎ 934 515 417
28. DIONISOS. València, 112 ☎ 932 260 049

29. EL CELLER DE MACONDO. Consellers, 4 ☎ 933 194 372

30. EL CHIRINGUITO ESCRIBÀ. Avinguda Litoral Mar, 42 ☎ 932 210 729

31. EL JAPONÉS. Passeig de la Concepció, 5 ☎ 934 870 621

32. EL PRINCIPAL. Provença, 286 ☎ 932 720 845

33. EL SALERO. Rec, 60 ☎ 933 198 022

34. ESCOLA DE RESTAURACIÓ. Muntaner, 70-72 ☎ 934 532 903

35. ESTRELLA DE PLATA. Pla de Palau, 9 ☎ 933 196 007

36. EUSKAL ETXEA. Placeta Montcada, 1-3 ☎ 933 102 185

37. FLASH-FLASH. La Granada del Penedés, 25 ☎ 932 370 990

38. FONT DE LLÚRIA. Roger de Llúria, 54 ☎ 934 878 404

39. FURACU. Girona, 52 ☎ 932 651 783

40. GAIG. Passeig Maragall, 402 ☎ 934 291 017 (not on map)

41. GORRIA. Diputació, 421 ☎ 932 327 857

42. GOVINDA. Plaça de la Vila de Madrid, 4 ☎ 933 187 729

43. HABANA BARCELONA. Escar, 1 ☎ 932 250 263

44. HAN IN JONG. Aribau, 32 ☎ 934 540 563

45. HERMANOS TOMÁS. Pare Pérez del Pulgar, 1 ☎ 933 457 148 (not on map)

46. HOSTAL EL PINTOR. Sant Honorat, 7 ☎ 933 014 065

47. IL BELLINI. Via Augusta, 201 ☎ 932 005 099

48. IL GIARDINETTO. Granada del Penedés, 22 ☎ 932 187 526

49. IRATI. Cardenal Casañas, 17 ☎ 933 023 084

50. JAUME DE PROVENÇA. Provença, 88 ☎ 933 227 931

51. KARAKALA. Torrent de l'Olla, 136 ☎ 934 156 686

52. LA CAMARGA. Aribau,117 ☎ 933 236 655

53. LA CANTINA. Gran de Gràcia, 167 ☎ 932 376 020

54. LA CABASSA. Brosolí, 1 ☎ 933 103 306

55. LA CARRETA. Balmes, 358 ☎ 934 185 784

56. LA LUNA DE ESTAMBUL. Avinguda Tarragona, 110 ☎ 933 232 565

57. LA MAISON DU LANGUEDOC ROUSSILLON. Pau Claris, 77 ☎ 933 010 498

58. LA MUSCLERIA. Mallorca, 290 ☎ 934 589 844

59. LA ROSA DEL DESIERTO. Plaça Narcís Oller, 7 ☎ 932 374 590

60. LA RUEDA. Rosselló, 266 ☎ 932 073 163

61. LA TABERNA DE ORIENTE. Torrent de l'Olla, 123 ☎ 934 156 077

62. LAS CUARTETAS. Santaló, 73 ☎ 932 017 934

63. LE CAFÉ BRISTOT. Muntaner, 161 ☎ 933 211 181

64. LE PETIT BERGERAC. Aribau, 41 ☎ 934 305 758

65. LES BRUIXES. Ramón y Cajal, 114 ☎ 932 842 343

66. LITTLE ITALY. Rec, 30 ☎ 933 197 973

67. LOS AÑOS LOCOS. Marià Cubí, 85 ☎ 932 096 915

68. LOS ASADORES. Avinguda Príncep d'Astúries, 4 ☎ 932 378 907

69. LUNGOMARE. Marina, 16-18 ☎ 932 210 428

70. MAITETXU. Balmes, 55 ☎ 933 235 965

71. MARGARITA BLUE. Josep A. Clavé, 6 ☎ 933 177 176

72. MEDULIO. Avinguda Príncep d'Astúries, 6 ☎ 932 173 868

73. MERLOT. Diputació, 381 ☎ 932 650 608

74. MESÓN MORRIÑA. Parlament, 46 ☎ 934 419 336

75. MESOPOTAMIA. Verdi, 65 ☎ 932 371 563

76. MÉXICO LINDO. Regàs, 35 ☎ 932 181 818

77. MOLINA CHARCUTERÍA. Plaça Molina, 1 ☎ 932 005 769
78. NEGRO. Avinguda Diagonal, 640. ☎ 934 059 444
79. NEICHEL. Beltrán i Rúzpide, 16 ☎ 932 038 408
80. NO ME QUITE PÁ. Marià Cubí, 192-194 ☎ 934 140 376
81. OT. Torres, 25 ☎ 932 847 752
82. PASSADÍS DEL PEP. Pla de Palau, 2 ☎ 933 101 021
83. PEKÍN. Rosselló, 202 ☎ 932 150 177
84. PEKÍN. Sant Antoni M. Claret, 500 ☎ 933 512 738
85. PITARRA. Avinyó, 56 ☎ 933 011 647
86. PLANET GREECE. París, 147 ☎ 934 102 821
87. POU DOLÇ. Baixada Sant Miquel, 6 ☎ 934 120 579
88. QUIMET & QUIMET. Poeta Cabanyes, 25 ☎ 934 423 142
89. RESTAURANT SET PORTES. Passeig Isabel II, 14 ☎ 933 193 033
90. RESTAURANT DEL TNC. Plaça de les Arts, 1 ☎ 933 065 729
91. RESTAURANTE LA FLACA. Villarroel, 227 ☎ 933 223 063
92. RÍAS DE GALICIA. Lleida, 7 ☎ 934 248 152
93. RÍO AZUL. Balmes, 92 ☎ 932 159 333
94. SANDWICH & FRIENDS. Passeig del Born, 27 ☎ 933 100 786
95. SANTA MARIA. Comerç, 17 ☎ 933 151 227
96. SANTIANGUIÑO. Buenos Aires, 2 ☎ 934 103 022
97. SATORU MIYANO. Ganduxer, 18 ☎ 934 143 104
98. SENYOR PARELLADA. Argenteria, 37 ☎ 933 105 094
99. SHILA. Aribau, 32 ☎ 934 540 563
100. SHOJIRO. Ros de Olano, 11 ☎ 934 146 548
101. SUSHI & NEWS. Santa Mònica, 2 bis ☎ 933 185 857
102. SUSHI-YA. Quintana, 4 ☎ 934 127 942
103. SYNDBAD. Aribau, 151 ☎ 934 197 041
104. TAIRA. Comerç, 7 ☎ 933 196 614
105. TÁKTIKA BERRI. València, 169 ☎ 934 534 759
106. TALAIA MAR. Marina, 16 ☎ 932 219 090
107. TANGUITO. València, 329 ☎ 934 576 937/934 591 151
108. THAÏ GARDENS. Diputació, 273 ☎ 934 879 898
109. TRAM-TRAM. Major de Sarrià, 121 ☎ 932 048 518 (not on map)
110. TUTUSAUS. Francesc Pèrez Cabrero, 5 ☎ 932 098 373/932 091 662
111. WOK & BOL. Diputació, 294 ☎ 933 027 675
112. YASHIMA. Avinguda Josep Tarradellas, 145 ☎ 934 190 697

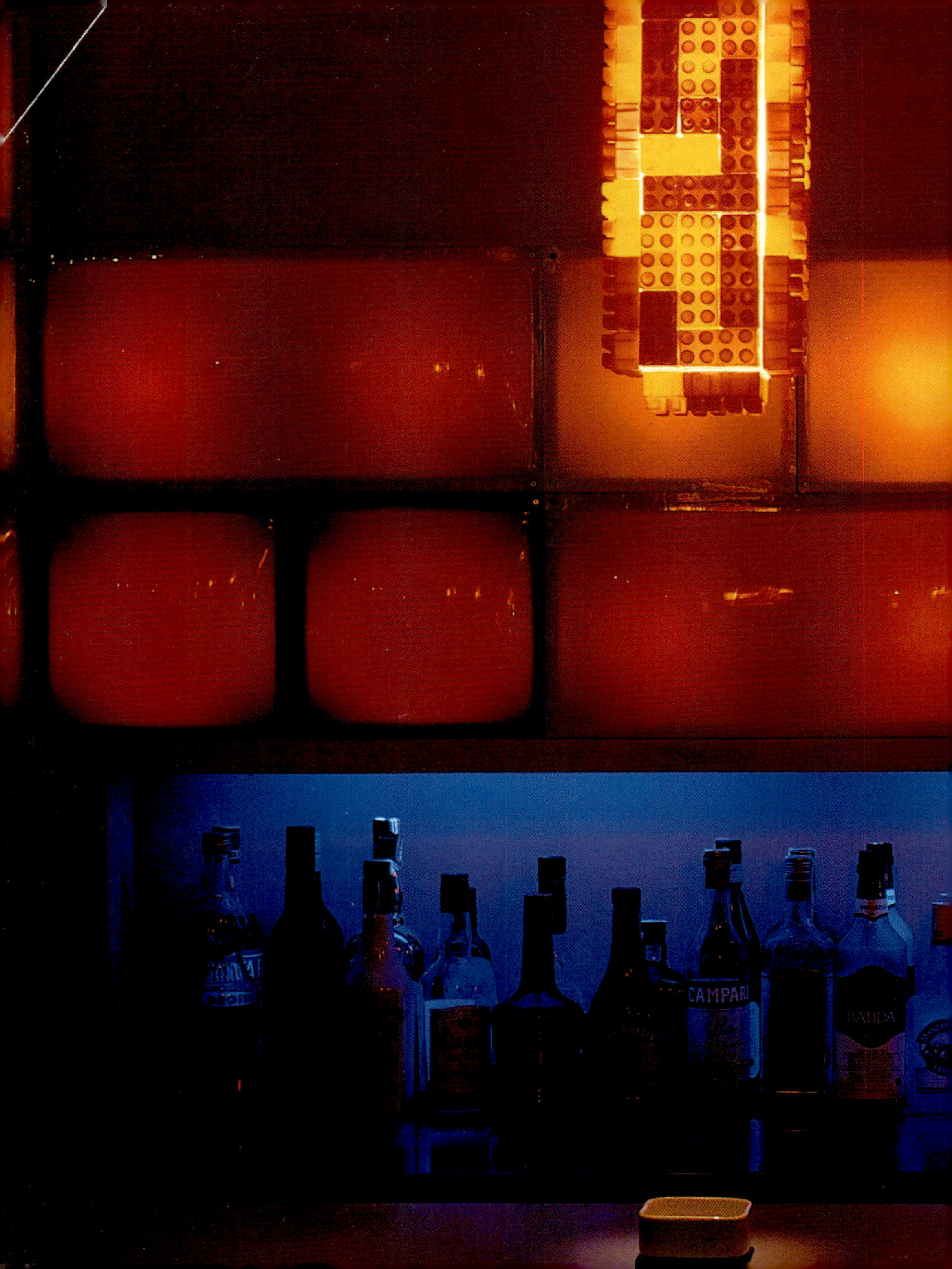
CAMPARI
BATIDA

Living night

Living night

Barcelona is famous for the wide variety of possibilities its night life offers. Given their open, Mediterranean, cosmopolitan nature, Barcelonans understand the city as an extension of their own house. Hence, the streets are alive with people chatting and strolling while they look for a place that suits them. This happens both night and day, and when it grows dark this constant bustle does not disappear. Quite the contrary: the streets with cocktail bars, the environs of the city's theaters, movie theaters, and concert halls, and of course the festivals, the discos, the party spots all see a constant flow of visitors out to enjoy whatever the night offers them.

Barcelona dines, drinks, and parties to the small hours of the morn. Its nighttime jumps especially briskly from Thursday till Saturday, the days with the most active nightlife. The closing hour of different establishments varies according to the activity. Music bars, for example, usually close their doors at three in the morning, while discotheques shut down between five and seven.

Night tends to begin with a good dinner and a drink at a music bar, then another one in a pub that stays open till dawn, and then on to dance for as long as the body can take it. Or else a concert might be preferred, or the discovery of some café theater... Or else the delights of small, welcoming spaces where aspiring artists perform. There are many possibilities.

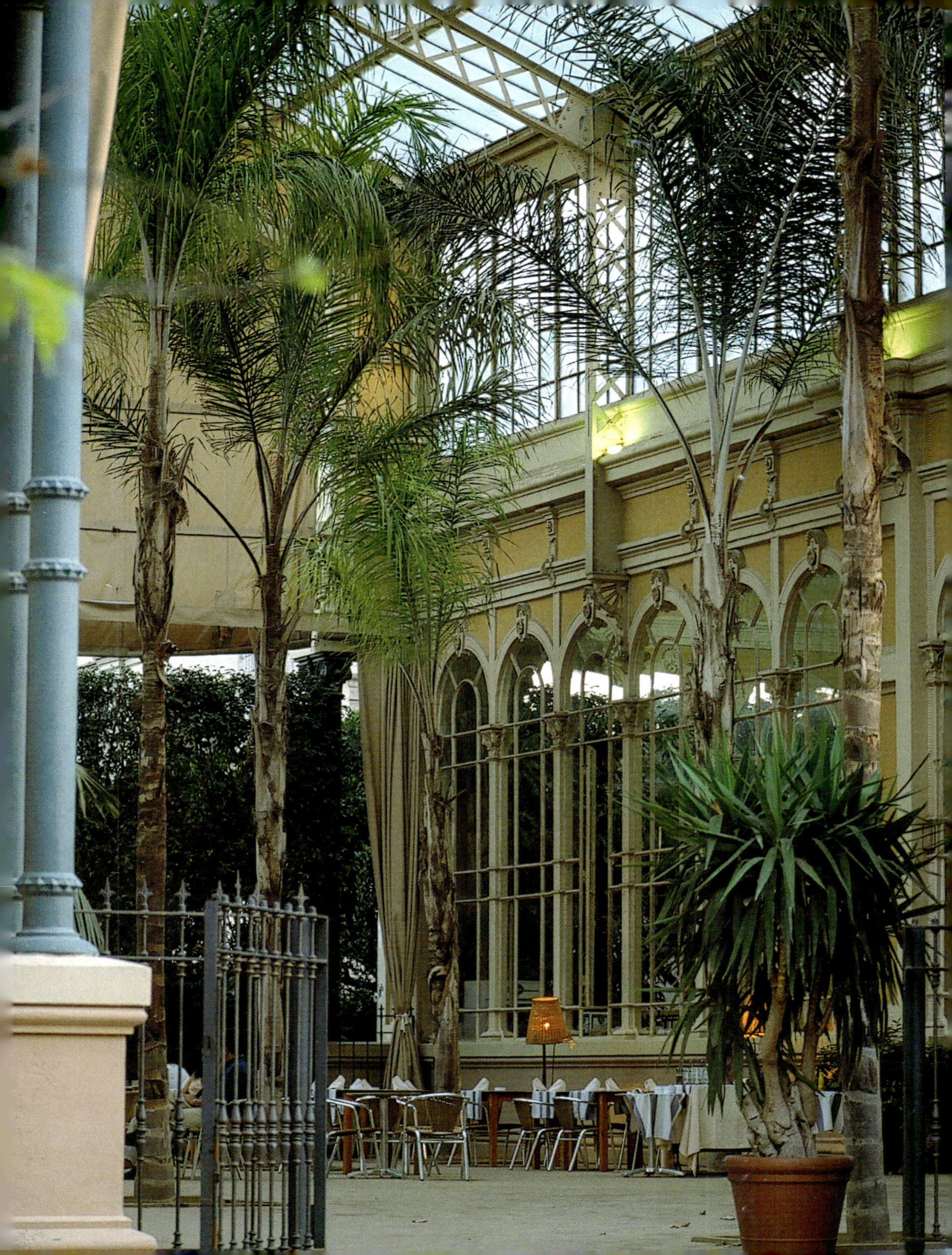

BARS

The bars of Barcelona are of all types, modern, noisy, warm, intimist, unique... They play an important role in the life of the city, both day and night. But it is when the sun goes down that they take on their really special role. The scene isn't limited to one single district, but is distributed all over the city, probably somewhat more visible in specific areas like the Barri Gòtic, Poble Nou, or the Born District, where the largest number of night spots are to be found.

In the Born, as has been mentioned, you'll find the city's most bohemian venues, many inspired by London's Soho, but also designer bars. Some of these are the Suborn, El Foro, or Abaixadors 10, this last being a locale that isn't easy to define since it organizes concerts, films, exhibitions, presentations, poetry readings... and an endless list of other activities. The more intellectual, modern places, open to new experiences, are in this neighborhood: Mudanzas, La Rosa de Foc, Kafka, or Borneo are some of the favorites.

The historical center and its environs, with more commercial and touristic streets, also transform and prepare themselves when the shutters go down. They are then ready to receive the nighttime crowds. The Barri Gòtic breathes a multicultural and carefree air, which means that there are spaces for all tastes. The Plaça Reial, the area's real nerve center, is astir with nightlife, with an infinite number of possibilities for all ages and styles. Having a drink in the Glaciar or the Pipa Club are two good ones, but not the only options. On another side of the

Located in the Poble Espanyol at Montjuïc, El Tablao de Carmen, named in homage to one of flamenco's legendary figures, Carmen Amaya, brims with the magic, the charm, and genius of flamenco in its cuisine of typical Andalusian dishes as well as in the tablao, where dance and singing performances are put on nightly.

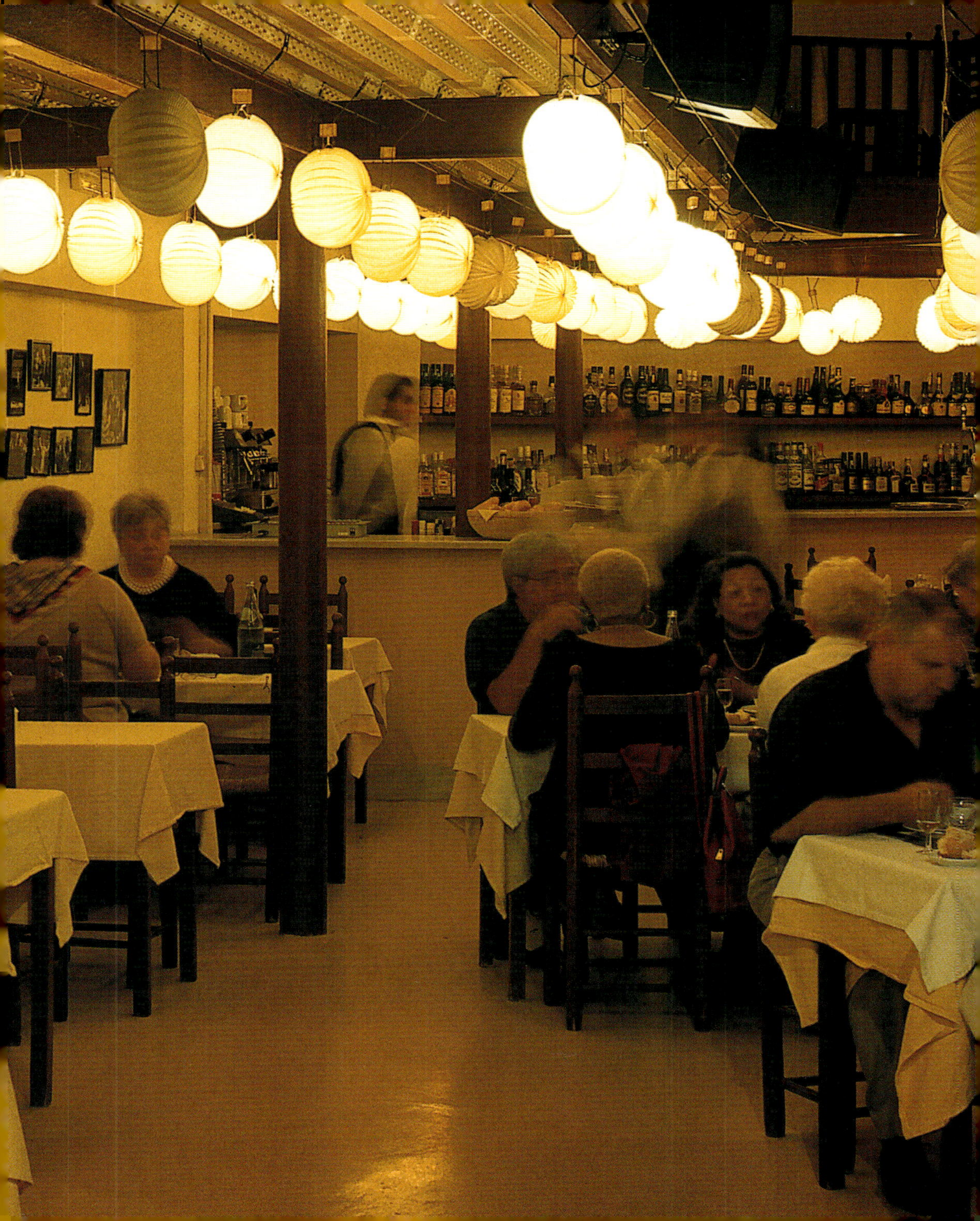

plaza is the Sidecar, an open space that programs all kinds of artistic and cultural activities, including musical events and dances. One of the venues currently popular is on a narrow street that gives onto this plaza. This is called the Café Royal, inaugurated by Hollywood Oscar-winner Pedro Almodóvar and one of the city's most "in" spots. In this area also is Karma, a disco with more than 20 years of life behind it and a neo-hippie, neo-grunge gauge. Al Limón Negro is another small but charming locale on one of those small streets. To the rhythms of jazz, folk, flamenco, or electronic, from the streets bordering the cathedral and the narrow side streets of the Barri Gòtic, small bars and cafés adapt themselves to every taste.

Heading seaward down the Rambla, the Maremàgnum and the Port Olímpic, inaugurated during the 1992 Olympic Games, await: large complexes with music bars, cocktail bars, karaokes, and discos.

Recently much in vogue and with a large nocturnal following, the Gràcia neighborhood maintains its popular flavor and has an immense number of bars and terraces open generally until three in the morning. There are (for example): Eldorado, L'Escenari-Teatreneu (cafeteria and bar inside the theater), El Café del Sol, Sol Soler, or Mond Bar (an establishment that took only two years to gain fame as a special venue dedicated to pop music, soul, techno pop, and sixties music).

The Eixample Quarter has its nighttime offering concentrated between the carrer Balmes, the carrer Aribau, and the carrer Muntaner. The great diversity of bar life here competes with that of the city's other districts, with rainbow flags in no small number of bars, greeting all and sundry with no bars on race, gender, or sexual orientation.

Poble Nou is a favorite area of the youngest crowd. The type of music and the decorating style are directed mostly to a population aged between 16 and 25. These are laid back locales, with a decor that may not be as carefully finished and where the price of drinks is relatively low.

The majority of these spots begin their activity on Tuesday, since Monday is often taken off by their personnel. In any case, those wishing to go out on any day of the week can always go to the Dot, a pure London style club that offers all types of music, funk, grunge, breakbeat.. It is not a large space but it has a lot of charm. Another place that opens every day of the week is the Moog, a small club dedicated to house and techno and that has a floor dedicated to electronic music and a chill-out space. The best DJs pass through here.

For electronic music and house aficionados, and those into the new scene in general, there are other unmissables: the Row, cosmopolitan and open, de rigueur for the most important DJs; La Paloma, a dance club that became mythical in Barcelona years ago and that offers Thursday nights where house and cool alternate. In a district with a great nocturnal leisure tradition, the popular Paral.lel, is the Nitsa, three rooms to enjoy techno

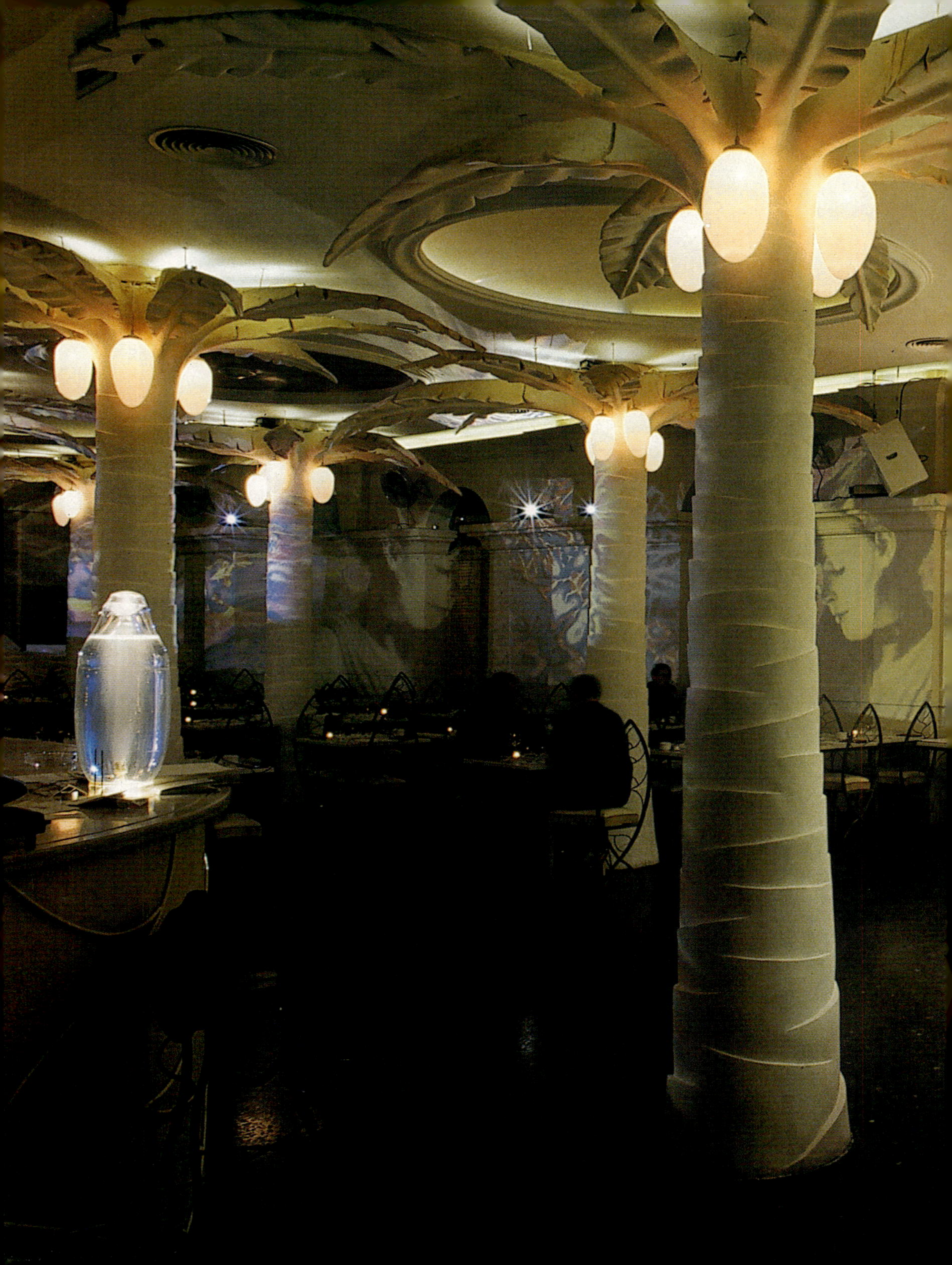

and house, a little bit louder, here, and also hip-hop and the latest pop. Another dancing space with a long tradition, La Cibeles, transforms itself on Friday's only into the Mond Club, offering DJ sessions you won't forget, live music, and a pop program.

The Astin and the Fonfone are other places with a young clientele, ideal for those looking for something different.

To decide where to go for a wild night, the best advice we can offer is that you choose the kind of activity the establishment specializes in. To begin the night, it's best to visit venues like El Café Que Pone Muebles Navarro, a name that translates to The Café With Navarro Furniture, which is what the building used to be, minus the "café": a furniture store. It is currently a warm, welcoming space where unique interior decoration, a great variety of armchairs, side chairs, sofas, tables, and lamps, highlights the locale's past for current visitors.

The Benidorm is another attractive spot to begin the night, and so is the Almirall, a modernista place of great prestige that has kept old style charm intact and which is like an invitation to pure cordiality. The Schilling is one of those cafés that found the secret to fame thanks to its northern European style decor. It is in what was once a knife factory, something many of its cosmopolitan clients are probably unaware of. La Bolsa is a bar that works, as its name (bourse, market) implies, like a stock market, the demand for different drinks making their

The Fonfone offers the best of funk, break beat, and even more recent musical forms. The Margarida Blue, along with its savory blend of Mexican and Mediterranean cuisine, offers after-midnight bar life.

prices vary. But there are still more locations to begin the night. La Fira, for the nostalgic, is a jumble of amusement park objets, mirrors, automata, roller coasters... These objects all have their story to tell, taking the visitor back to a magical world. The same might be said of El Bosc de les Fades (Enchanted Forest) beside the Museu de Cera. This is a place that has been imaginatively decorated on the fantasy of the land of children's stories, inviting us into the dream world. The London Bar is a real classic in Barcelona's night life. The Zsa-Zsa has the ambience of a cocktail bar to the rhythm of mestizo airs and salsa rhythms, and in the Marsella you can enjoy a drink while a seer reads your future on the cards. Those who like kitsch environments won't want to miss La Bata de Boatiné, and those who prefer to go to see a trapeze act should go into the Fussina some Thursday. Fun is Back is also a nice venue for a first quiet drink with the best house sounds in the background, and on Wednesdays and Thursdays from the end of June it programs theme parties. The Fonfone is indispensable to the musical scene, or Club 22, with alternative music sessions, jazz, hard house, are two other good spots to hit early in the evening.

> The nocturnal scene constantly renews itself. The latest venues provide a classy musical selection with the best DJs, both national and international, a good lure for landing an audience on the cutting edge.

living night 73

discotheques

Barcelona will offer you veritable dancing sanctuaries combining tradition and modernity and catering to all tastes. In contrast to what occurs in the music bars, however, the dancing joints have an established cover charge.

Bikini and Up & Down are two classic locales in Barcelona's nightlife. Both are located uptown; both are popular with celebrities. They began in the 60s and after some ups and downs and a few changes have adapted themselves to today's market. Bikini is, in addition to a live music bar (like the Jamboree, for another example) one of Spain's mythical clubs. It has seen performances by people like Ella Fitzgerald or Chat Baker. Currently, the program is all jazz, from the most classical to the most recent. After the sets, the locale becomes one of the city's most-frequented discos thanks to its dedication to the new and the novel. La Boîte is another classic. Open since 1990, it offers live performances by name musicians and also a disco with the best dance music and funk. Disco fans of 80s soundtracks should go to Velvet. A select set gets together in Luna Mora and Las Torres de Ávila. Those looking for fashion style will want to poke their noses into Otto Zutz or Music Box Beethoven. Hits Box, an 80s revival locale, is 4-D; in the Nayandeï or in Starwinds (both in the Maremàgnum complex) they spin the most danceable up-to-the-microsecond rhythms. These are the places that never let you down.

To dance to good pop, dance music, and funk, the Costa Breve. At Baja Beach Club, lovers of artificial beach-

Many legendary dance clubs in the city have renewed their nighttime offer of entertainment by adding DJs. Most days they operate as dance halls with live bands, but one or two days a week they have different kinds of musical events aimed at a younger audience.

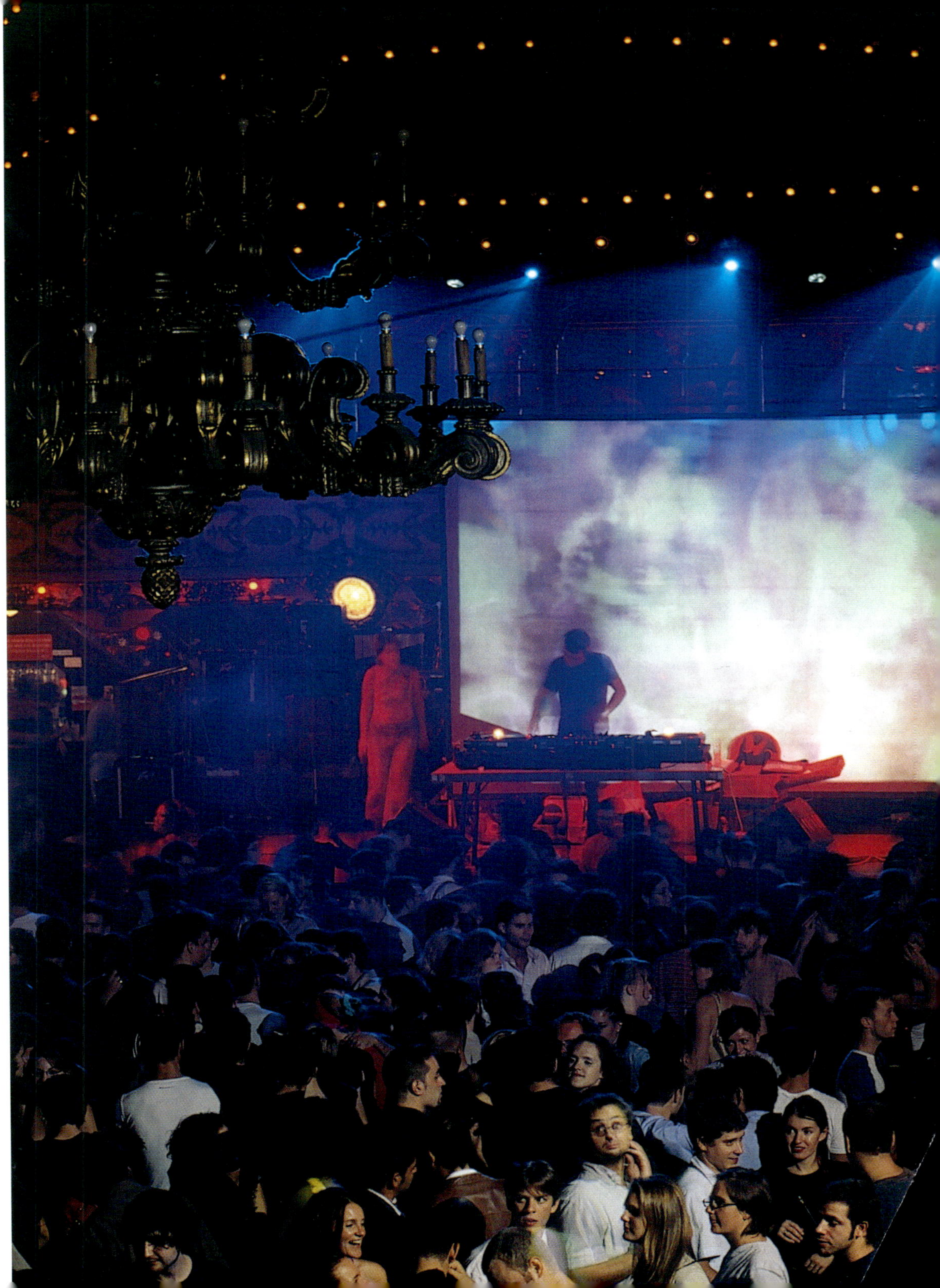

es will find themselves in paradise. And for the youngest movers, Bóveda or Illusion. In El Sol you'll find it easy to forget your troubles dancing to today's beat. Apolo discotheque is hereby recommended to the most alternative crowd. It is in an old dance spot that has become one of the city's most up-to-date, offering the best electronic music DJs. The KGB, in Gràcia, is open to all, from the youngest to 30-some. Antilla Barcelona is aimed at salsa lovers. Today's Razzmatazz made the dream of many Barcelonans come true by keeping some of the mythical Zeleste alive. It not only offers live music concerts, it offers them in the oldest such venue in Poble Nou. Les Enfants, La Terrazza, and Discotèque are three of the most fashionable cutting-edge "discos." The same can be said of Fish, which opened inside a recently inaugurated gaming megacenter exclusively dedicated to entertainment, Heron City.

For more specific crowds the city also offers Magic, one of the last pure hard-rock redoubts; Mephisto, for aficionados of heavy; Arena, a gay disco.

open since 1904, La Paloma is Barcelona's dance club par excellence. Its modernist decor was recently discovered by a more contemporary crowd, which makes it one of the key spots in the city for house late Thursday nights.

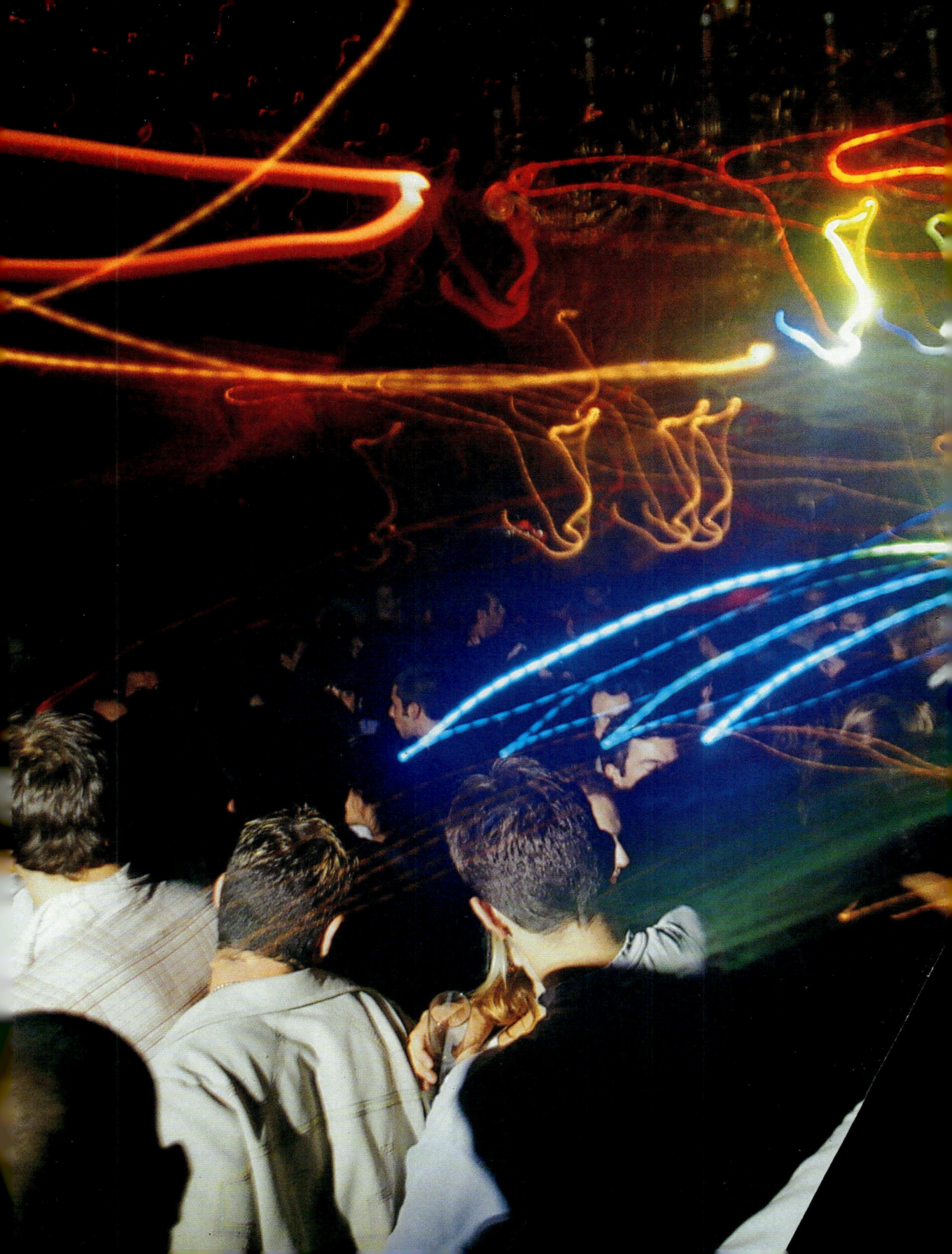

other alternatives

Those who enjoy **live music**, La Cova del Drac is a must. In addition to its live jazz sessions, the stage in this locale is used for such activities as poetry readings and tap dancing shows. Live music is available at the Harlem Jazz Club and the Jazz Sí Club, with practically all jazz and flamenco styles heard. At Luz de Gas, an old dance hall that was refurbished to adapt to new times, live music plus disco is on offer. The Garatge programs alternative music concerts for a younger crowd, but at the end of the session the beat goes on with a DJ.

Hot rhythm lovers and lovers of **folk music** have not been forgotten. In places such as El Atxé, Cuban rhythms pervade; El Copetín, Mojito Bar, and Samba Brasil have hotter tropical notes and teach the secrets of the samba, the lambada, and salsa.

Barcelona has always been into **Flamenco**, an art popular with many audiences. Special tablaos offer live Flamenco. Los Tarantos is famous for high quality shows, so is the recently inaugurated Las Lolas Club, with voice and dance performances every Sunday, films, and a large number of activities related to the world of Flamenco. El Patio Andaluz offers dinner and show in the same locale, in a good ambience and along the same lines as El Tablao de Carmen, dedicated to the mythical dancer of genius, the bailaora Carmen Amaya. Another of the great spaces dedicated to Flamenco is El Cordobés. Among other activities, this locale organizes singing contests. Passing through the doors of one of these venues is an entire adventure, as the fiesta is assured.

For the not so young or those who miss old-**time dance spots**, there are still some venues in the city. One of the most emblematic of these is La Paloma, with magical decor dating back to 1904 and in keeping with the pasodobles, tangos, chachachas and boleros that can still be danced every day except Thursday, when renowned DJs are on and a different kind of clientele comes in. La Cibeles also changes clientele, but on Fridays, the rest of the week it dedicates its floor to classical rhythms. Tango, Sutton, Época, are three other locales that revive rhythms heard less these days.

During the hottest months of the year, the **carpas** and **terraces** win out. The carpas appeared only in recent years and are locations that in summer become open air discos. The most notable are Firestiu, Torre Melina, and Carpe Diem. The terraces are ideal for beginning the night when the heat bears down. They are distributed throughout the city: uptown, in the Tibidabo district; downtown, around Plaça Reial, Gràcia, or the Port Olímpic. Some examples: the legendary Zurich, Tèxtil Café, Los Tilos, El Café de la Ópera, Mirabé.

Those who prefer the setting of typical **Irish pub**s might want to try the Irish Winds, an Irish setting with live Celtic music. In The Clansman, the best beer combines with Celtic music. The Quiet Man is another much-frequented locale where live music may be enjoyed. The Flann O'Brien, a genuine Irish pub, and the George & Dragon, are ideal for those who wish to practice English.

Karaokes enjoyed a great success at the beginning of the 90s and although the boom is no longer as spectacular as it once was, there are still a good number of locales that offer this type of activity. Those who want to try their luck in the world of song, imitate their favorite singers, or simply spend a fun night singing or listening will have a good time in A Viva Voz, U-Piano Bar, Star Factory, or Weekend.

Gay bars and **discos** proliferate throughout the city. The Eixample District has recently seen the opening of such a wide number of gay bars that it has been rebaptized as Gaixample by the gay community. All of these establishments are notable for their openness to mixed crowds. Satanassa is the essence of cutrelux (kitschluxe) and an institution in its own right in nighttime Barcelona. It offers lively music in a singular ambience. Another bar with a long tradition is Martin's. Dietrich as well as Metro are two obligatory classics in the gay scene, and they share a major role along with other, newer places like Salvation, La Diva, La Concha del Barrio Chino, or Miranda.

Those wishing to keep going once all the bars and discos have closed and the sun is coming up might go on to some of the city's **after-hours** venues. These are characterized by the policy of opening their doors from six or seven o'clock in the morning and closing in the early afternoon. Examples are Tijuana, Guantanamera, Member's, or Bunker. They all offer energetic morning sessions to the most daring and awake.

LA VERÓNICA

Café del Sol

GUINNESS
Molly's Fair City
WINES · SPIRITS · ALE
B

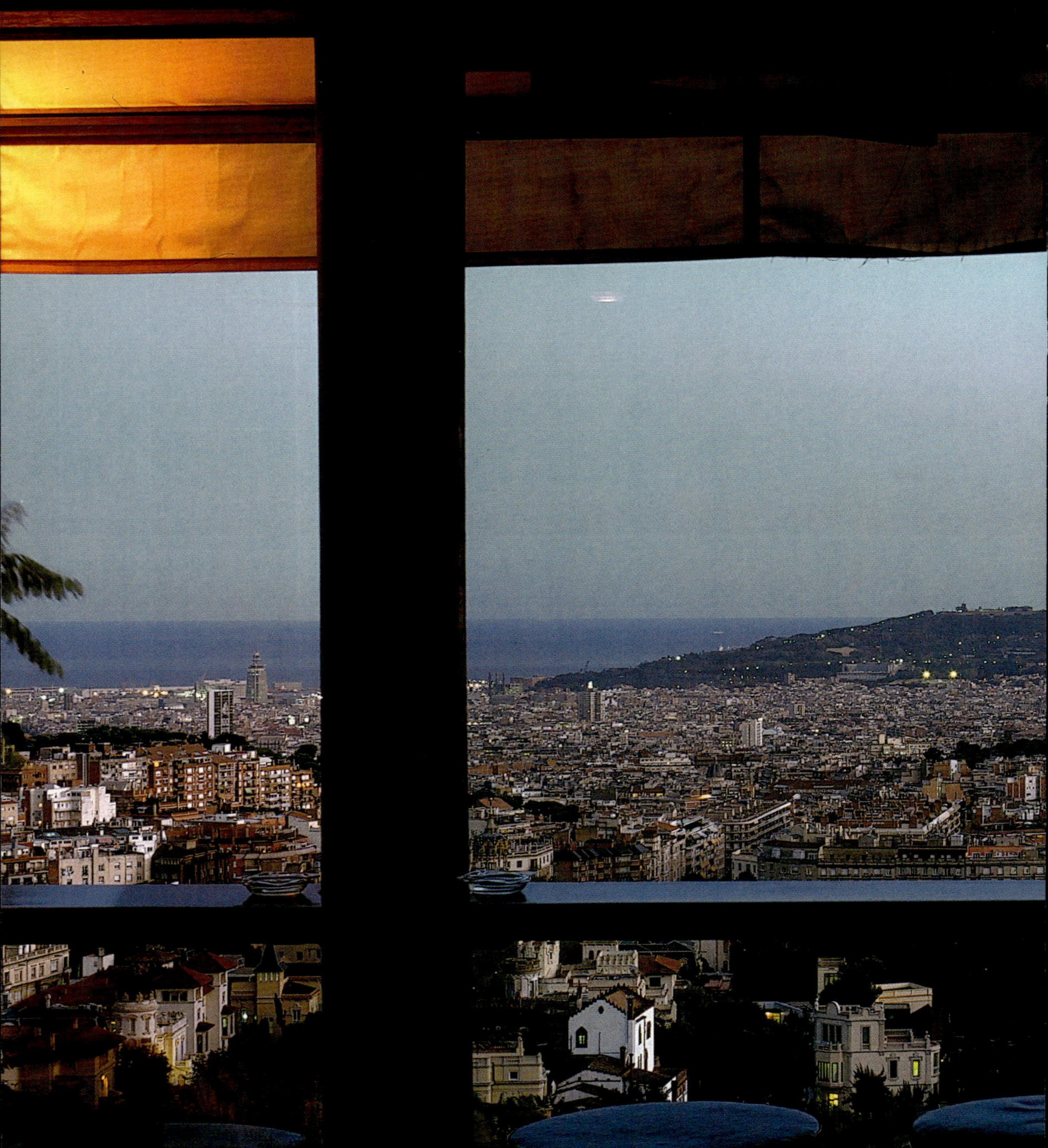

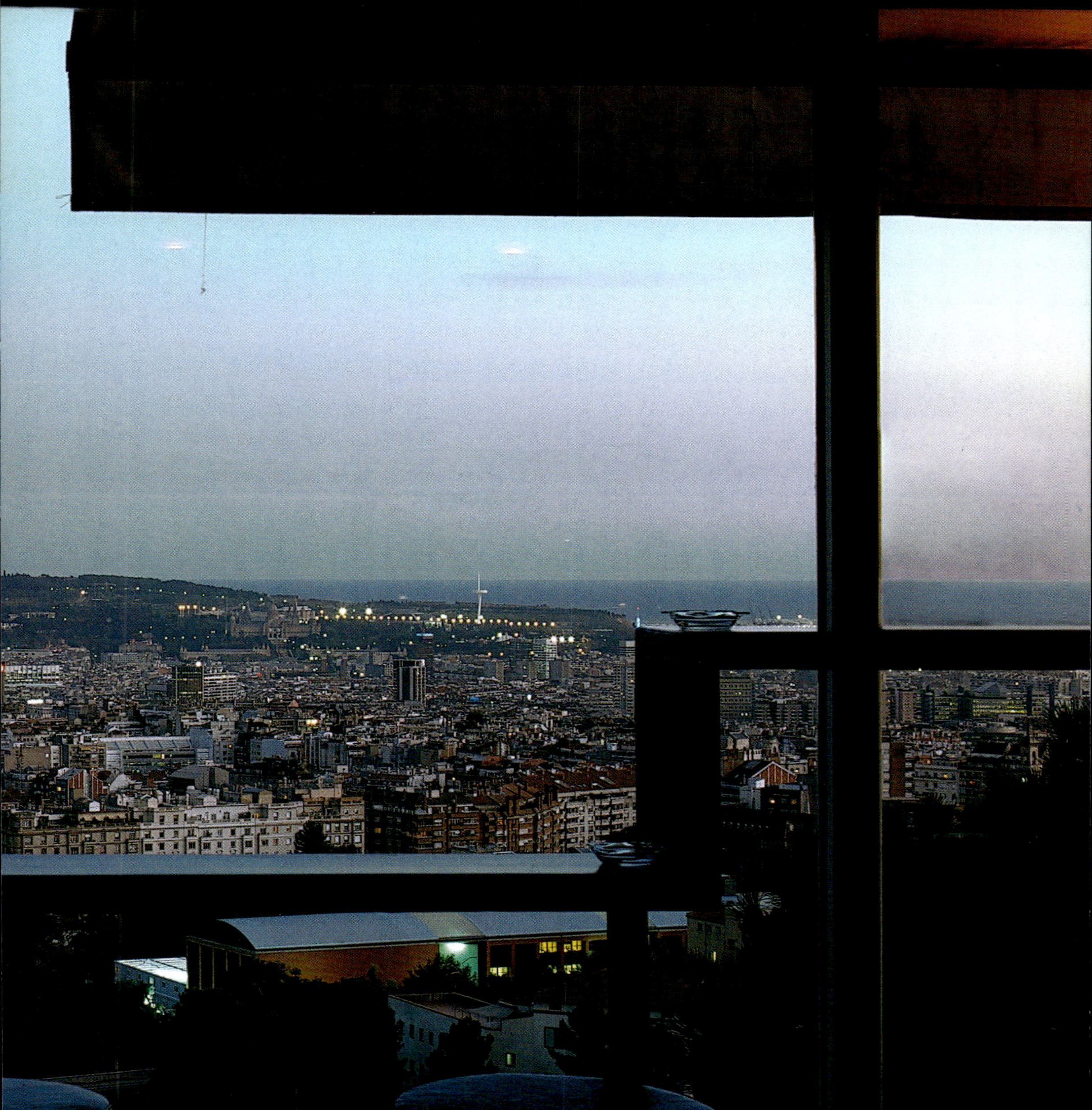

graphic design

Vanguardist clips, fragments of reality tinged with creativity, provocation, or a gamut of influences are some of the concepts that define the new and suggestive proposals in the field of graphic design stimulating Barcelona.

La Paloma
PALACIO DEL BAILE

LA PALOMA: TIGRE 27 • TEL.: 301 68 97
08001 BARCELONA
OFICINAS: PALOMA, 15 D
TEL.: 317 79 94 • FAX 317 72 25

republica
under the station

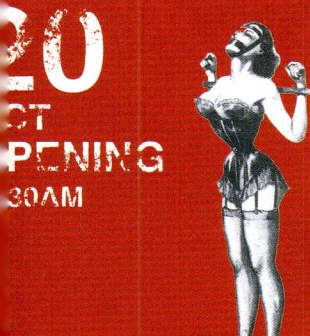

20
CT
PENING
30AM

club 22

abierto everyday de 11h. a 3h.   entrada libre dos salas (side A-side B)

www.newchoiceproductions.com/e

SEPTIEMBRE 2001

domingos - lunes sesiones lounge

c/ nou de la rambla 22   colabora salsitas   produce OCTOPUS

Fun is back

SEPTIEMBRE 2001

rbla. cataluña, nº 2-4
de 1 a 6 h

produce OCTOPUSSY
colabora SALSITAS
CITY HALL
diseño NCP

MOOG BARCELONA

OBERT TOTES LES NITS DE 12 H A 5.00 H
OPEN ALL NIGHTS FROM 12 H TO 5.00 H

DISCOUNT

FINS A LES 2 H.
1200 PTS. + CONSUMICIÓ

BEFORE 2 H.
1200 PTS. + FREEDRINK

ARC DEL TEATRE 3
08002 BARCELONA

NOU DE LA RAMB
ARC DEL TEATR
MOOG

29. EL COPETÍN. Passeig del Born, 19
30. EL CORDOBÉS. Rambla, 35 ☎ 933 175 711
31. EL FORO. Princesa, 53 ☎ 933 101 020
32. EL PATIO ANDALUZ. Aribau, 242
    ☎ 932 093 378/932 689 070
33. EL SOL. Villarroel, 216 ☎ 932 378 658
34. EL TABLAO DE CARMEN. Poble Espanyol
    ☎ 933 256 895/934 254 616
35. ELDORADO. Plaça del Sol, 4 ☎ 932 373 696
36. ÉPOCA. Gran Via, 322 ☎ 933 253 870
37. FIRESTIU. Av. Reina M. Cristina, s/n (june, july, august)
38. FISH. Passatge Andreu, edifici Mar, 2ª i 3ª planta. Heron City
    (not on map)
39. FLANN O'BRIEN. Casanova, 264 ☎ 932 011 606
40. FONFONE. Escudellers, 24 ☎ 933 171 424
41. FUN IS BACK. Rambla de Catalunya, 2-4
42. FUSE. Roger de Llúria, 40 ☎ 933 017 499
43. FUSSINA. Fusina, 6 ☎ 933 100 667
44. GARATGE. Pallars, 195 ☎ 933 091 438
45. GEORGE & DRAGON. Diputació, 269 ☎ 934 881 765
46. GLACIAR. Plaça Reial, 3 ☎ 933 021 163
47. GUANTANAMERA. Avinguda Meridiana, 140
48. HARLEM JAZZ CLUB. Comtessa de Sobradiel, 8
    ☎ 933 100 755
49. HERON CITY. Passatge Andreu Nin, s/n
    ☎ 902 333 231 (not on map)
50. HITS BOX. Maremàgnum, local 104 ☎ 932 258 041
51. ILLUSION. Lepant, 408 ☎ 933 473 600
52. IRISH WINDS. Maremàgnum, local 202
    ☎ 932 258 187
53. JAMBOREE. Plaça Reial, 17 ☎ 933 017 564
54. JAZZ SÍ CLUB. Requesens, 2 ☎ 933 290 020
55. KAFKA. Fusina, 7 ☎ 933 100 526
56. KARMA. Plaça Reial, 10 ☎ 933 025 680
57. KGB. Ca l'Alegre de Dalt, 55 ☎ 932 105 906
58. L'ESCENARI-TEATRENEU. Terol, 26-28
    ☎ 932 844 896
59. LA BATA DE BOATINÉ. Robador, 18
60. LA BOÎTE. Avinguda Diagonal, 477 ☎ 933 191 789
61. LA BOLSA. Tuset, 17 ☎ 932 412 533
62. LA CIBELES. Còrsega, 363 ☎ 934 573 877
63. LA CONCHA DEL BARRIO CHINO. Guàrdia, 14
    ☎ 933 024 118
64. LA COVA DEL DRAC. Vallmajor, 33 ☎ 932 007 032
65. LA DIVA. Diputació, 172 ☎ 934 546 398
66. LA FIRA. Provença, 171
67. LA PALOMA. Tigre, 27 ☎ 933 016 897
68. LA ROSA DE FOC. Antic de Sant Joan, 12
    ☎ 933 195 171
69. LA TERRAZZA. Avinguda Marqués de Comillas, s/n
    ☎ 933 187 980
70. LAS LOLAS CLUB. Plaça Reial, 17 ☎ 933 183 067
71. LAS TORRES DE ÁVILA. Avinguda Marquès de Comillas, 25 ☎ 934 249 309
72. LES ENFANTS. Guàrdia, 3 ☎ 934 120 048
73. LONDON BAR. Nou de la Rambla, 34 ☎ 933 185 261
74. LOS TARANTOS. Plaça Reial, 17 ☎ 933 183 067
75. LOS TILOS. Passeig dels Til·lers ☎ 932 037 546
    (not on map)
76. LUNA MORA. Ramon Trias Fargas, s/n ☎ 932 216 161
77. LUZ DE GAS. Muntaner, 246 ☎ 932 097 711
78. MAGIC. Passeig Picasso, 40 ☎ 933 107 267

79. MAREMÀGNUM. Moll d'Espanya, s/n ☎ 902 333 231
80. MARGARITA BLUE. Josep A. Clavé, 6 ☎ 933 177 176
81. MARSELLA. Sant Pau, 65
82. MARTIN'S. Passeig de Gràcia, 130 ☎ 932 187 167
83. MEMBER'S. Sèneca, 3 ☎ 932 371 204
84. MEPHISTO. Lutxana, 33 ☎ 933 091 315
85. METRO. Sepúlveda, 185 ☎ 933 235 227
86. MIRABÉ. Manuel Arnús, 2 ☎ 934 340 035 (not on map)
87. MIRANDA. Casanova, 30 ☎ 934 535 249
88. MOJITO BAR. Maremàgnum ☎ 933 528 746/932 258 014
89. MOND BAR. Plaça del Sol, 21
90. MOND CLUB. Còrsega, 363 ☎ 932 720 910
91. MOOG. Arc del Teatre, 3 ☎ 933 185 966
92. MUDANZAS. Vidrieria, 15 ☎ 933 191 137
93. MUSIC BOX BEETHOVEN. Beethoven, 15 ☎ 933 620 200; Avinguda Diagonal, 618 ☎ 932 093 589
94. NATANDEÏ. Maremàgnum, local 203 ☎ 932 258 010
95. NITSA. Nou de la Rambla, 113 ☎ 933 010 090
96. OTTO ZUTZ. Lincoln, 15 ☎ 932 380 722
97. PIPA CLUB. Plaça Reial, 3 ☎ 933 024 732
98. POBLE ESPANYOL. Avinguda Marquès de Comillas, 25 ☎ 933 257 866
99. PORT OLÍMPIC. Passeig Marítim del Port Olímpic
100. RAZZMATAZZ. Almogàvers, 122; Pamplona, 88 ☎ 933 208 200
101. REPÚBLICA. Marquès d'Argentera, 6 (Estació de França) ☎ 933 000 417
102. ROW. Rosselló, 208 ☎ 932 375 405
103. SALSITAS. Nou de la Rambla, 22 ☎ 933 180 840
104. SALVATION. Ronda Sant Pere, 19-21 ☎ 933 180 686
105. SAMBA BRASIL. Lepant, 297 ☎ 934 561 798
106. SATANASSA. Aribau, 27 ☎ 934 510 052
107. SCHILLING. Ferran, 23 ☎ 933 176 787
108. SIDECAR. Heures, 4-6 ☎ 933 021 586
109. SOL SOLER. Plaça del Sol, 13
110. STAR FACTORY. Balmes, 187 ☎ 932 370 944
111. STARWINDS. Terrassa Golf Maremàgnum ☎ 932 258 121
112. SUBORN. Ribera, 18 ☎ 933 101 110
113. SUTTON. Tuset, 13 ☎ 934 144 217/932 720 910
114. TANGO. Diputació, 94 ☎ 933 253 770
115. TÈXTIL CAFÉ. Montcada, 12 ☎ 932 682 598
116. THE CLANSMAN. Vigatans, 13 ☎ 933 197 169
117. THE QUIET MAN. Marquès de Barberà, 11 ☎ 934 121 219
118. TIJUANA. Passeig Marítim, 34 ☎ 932 254 963
119. TORRE MELINA. Torre Melina, s/n ☎ 934 146 362 (not on map)
120. UP & DOWN. Numància, 179 ☎ 932 055 194
121. U-PIANO BAR. Aragó, 221 ☎ 934 548 140
122. VELVET. Balmes, 161 ☎ 932 176 714
123. WEEKEND. Diputació, 365 ☎ 932 465 507
124. ZSA-ZSA. Rosselló, 156 ☎ 934 538 566
125. ZURICH. Pelai, 39 ☎ 933 179 153

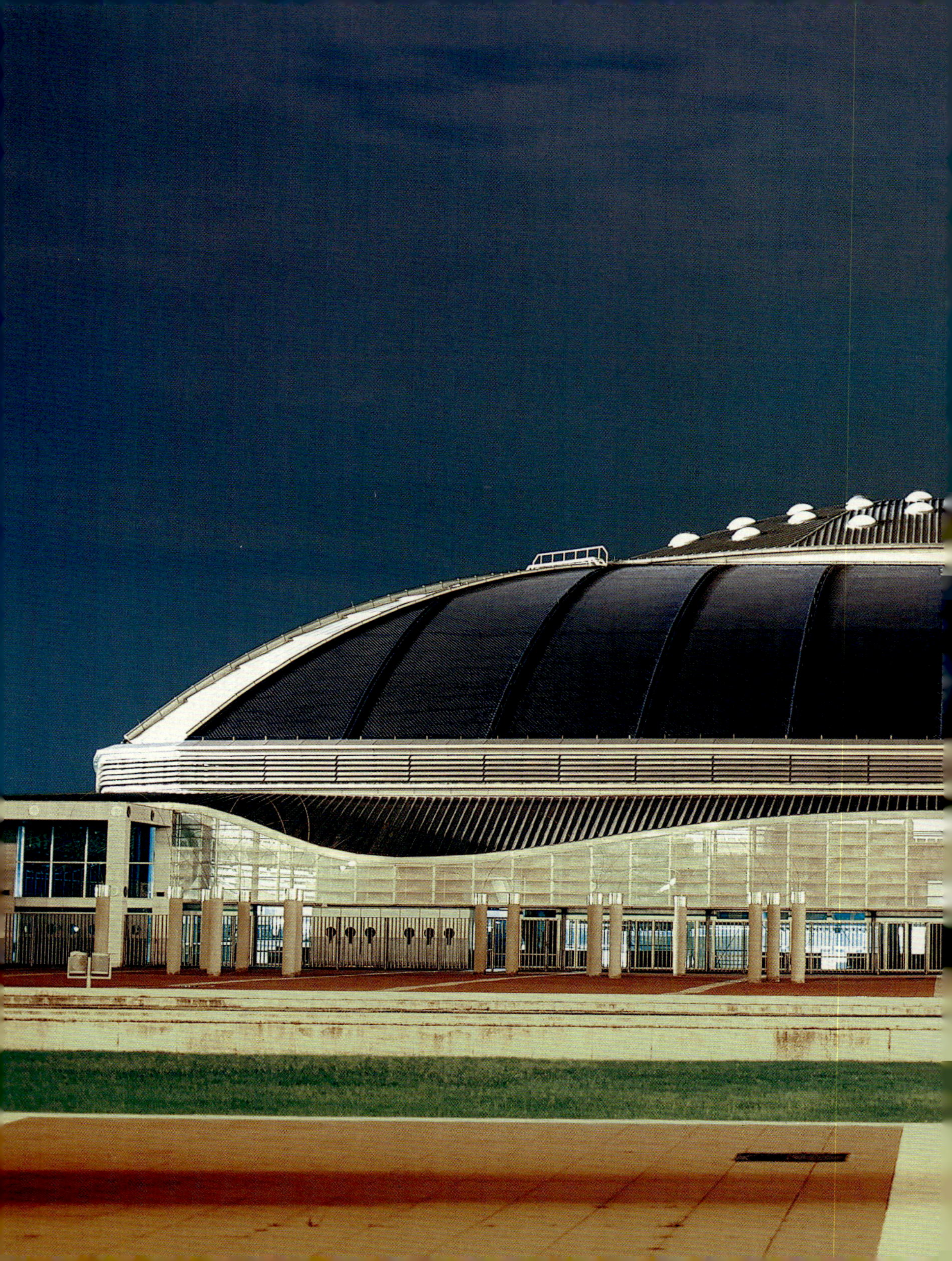

nighttime entertainment

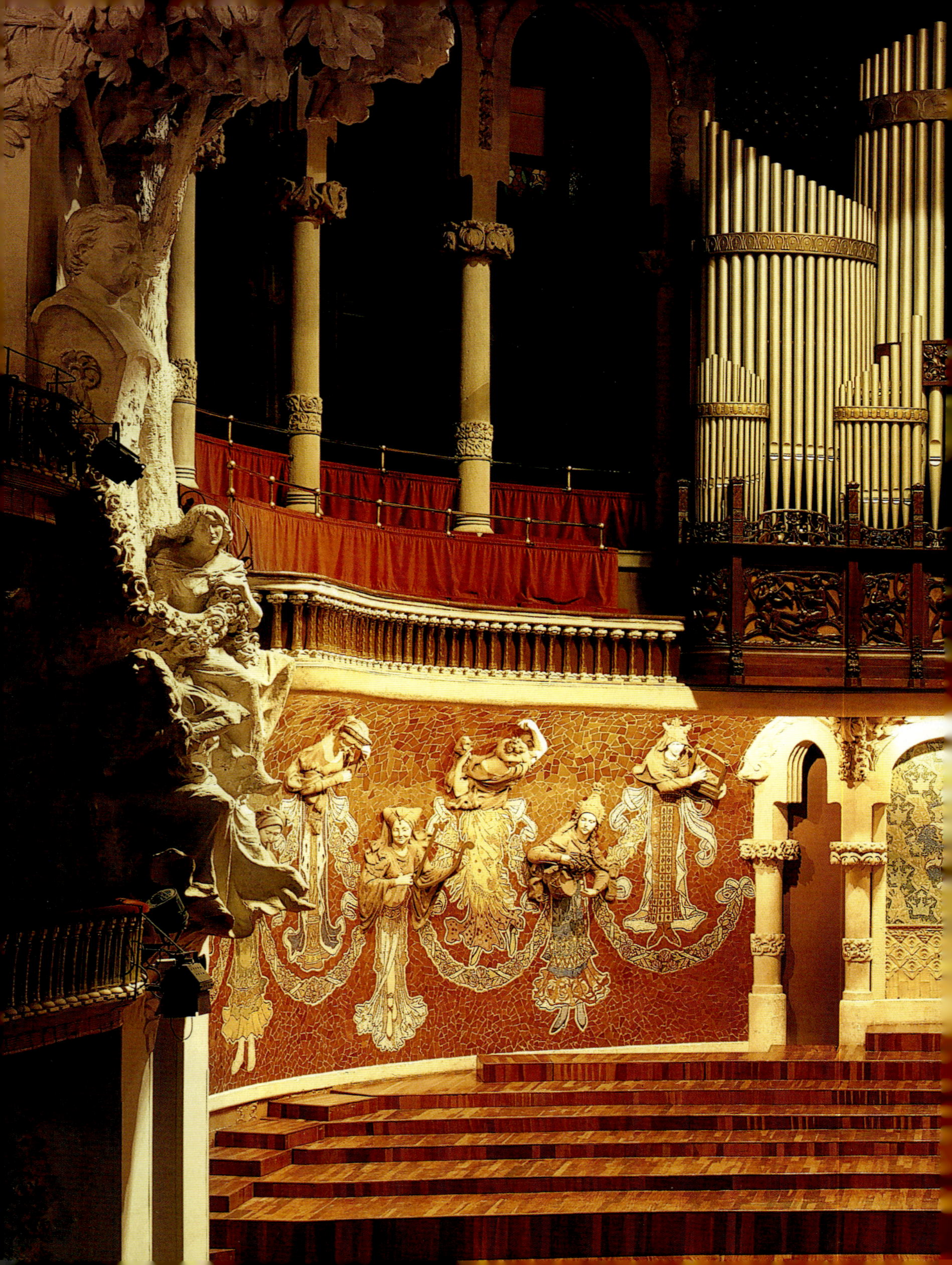

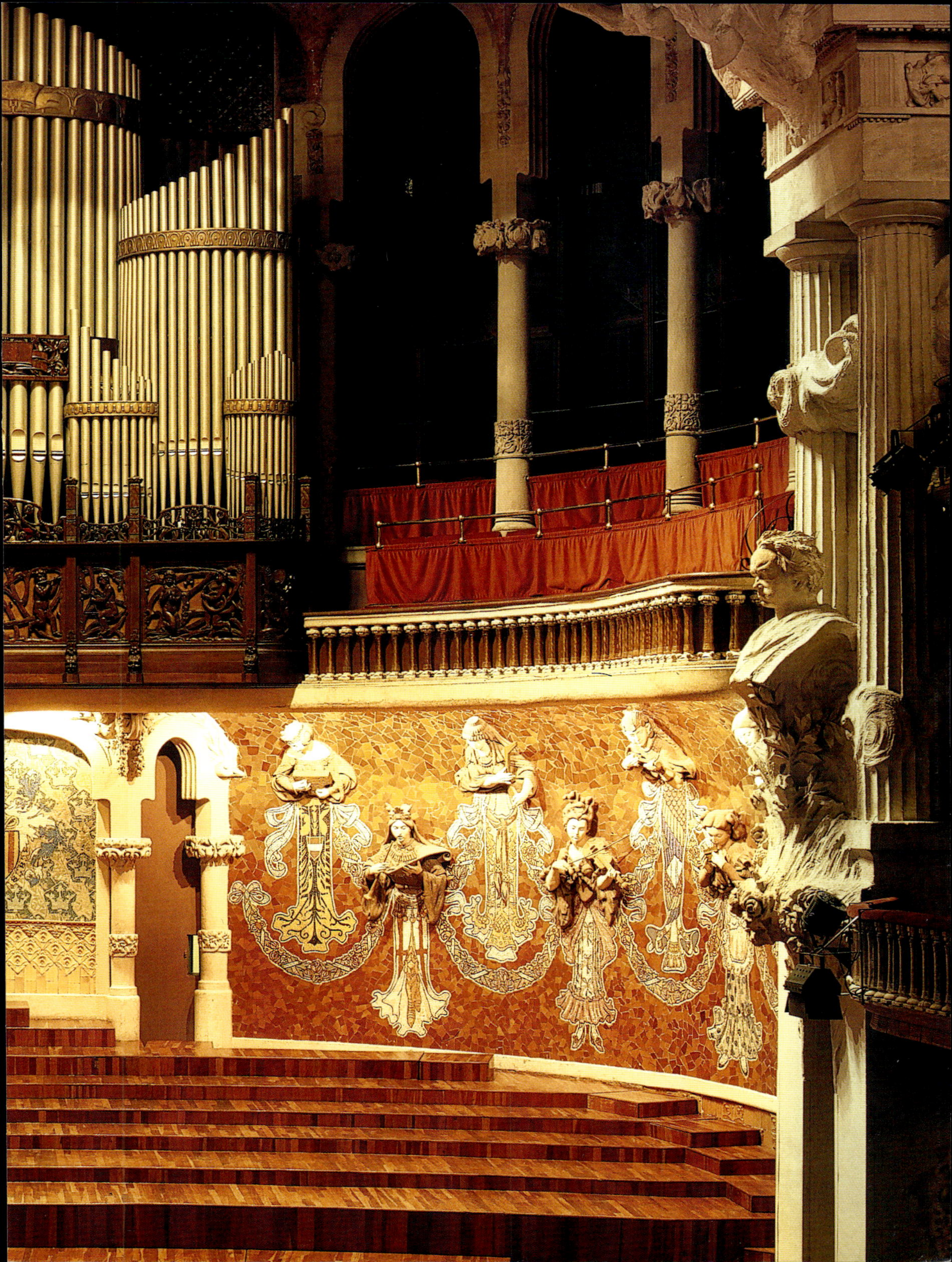

catering not only to classical music but also–thanks to its good acoustics— to concerts of other musical genres and styles.

Still another way of listening to good music is at the different festivals programmed during the year. An example is the "Músiques del Món" (Musics of the World) sponsored by the Fundació La Caixa; the BAM that coincides with the Festival of the Mercè (Barcelona's patron saint), with music in the streets and the plazas and other less habitual places like the Estació de França or Barcelona Cathedral; the "Festival de Músiques Contemporànies de Barcelona"; the Sónar, which, with the arrival of fair weather sets Barcelona moving to the beat of electronic music; and of course Flamenco and jazz festivals, among other types.

We should also remember that in addition to all the aforementioned activities there are many musical bars that program, from time to time, performances by less well-known or newer artists seeking their opportunity and also new bands and other groups. If music is inseparable from the life of Barcelonans, the **theatrical arts** are no less important. Myriad theaters and movie theaters are to be found in the city and this is hardly surprising if we reflect on the fact that these are the preferred forms of artistic expression for Barcelona's citizens.

The theater and movie circuit that make it possible to admire the best national and international acting which is programmed in Barcelona is extensive and varied. New spaces that provide an offering that programs alter-

The Palau de la Música de Barcelona is considered to be one of the highest exponents of Catalan modernisme (Art Nouveau style). Lluís Domenèch i Montaner was the architect commissioned to design the palau, in this style, and the building was classified as a UNESCO World Heritage in 1997.

native theater coexist side by side with large traditional theaters and with café-theaters or music halls. Definitively, this is prestige theater that is becoming known throughout Spain and that currently provides performances in more than 40 locations.

Something similar is true regarding the city's musical proposals, also programmed for many different festivals and theater cycles throughout the year. Probably the best known of these is the Festival d'Estiu del Grec (Greek theater summer festival) held at the Greek theater on Montjuïc, (a reproduction of an ancient Greek theater) as well as numerous stages in the city offering a summer season full of theater, dance, and music. The theatrical heart of the city is on the Avinguda Paral.lel, concentrating a great many of the different types of theater establishments that have come into being in the long history of the tradition in Barcelona. There are, for example, to name three of the major ones, the Teatre Victoria, the Teatre Apolo, and the Teatre Condal. In the city center, not far from the Paral.lel, more theaters are to be found, the Teatre Romea, the Goya, Novedades, Teatre Principal, Borràs and the Tivoli, to name only a few. Leaving the center and continuing on into the Gracia district, where a larger offering is to be found, we might consider the Teatre Lliure, l'Espai, Teatreneu or the Jove Teatre Regina. There are also the new Teatre Nacional de Catalunya, the Mercat de les Flors and the Institut del Teatre, the three stage complexes in the project "Ciutat del Teatre" (Theater City). Alternative and independent or expe-

In the wake of the devastating fire that partly destroyed it in 1994, the Gran Teatre del Liceu, Barcelona's opera house, reopened its doors in October 1999, after nearly five years of careful reconstruction. The result: a modern theater with the same durable spirit.

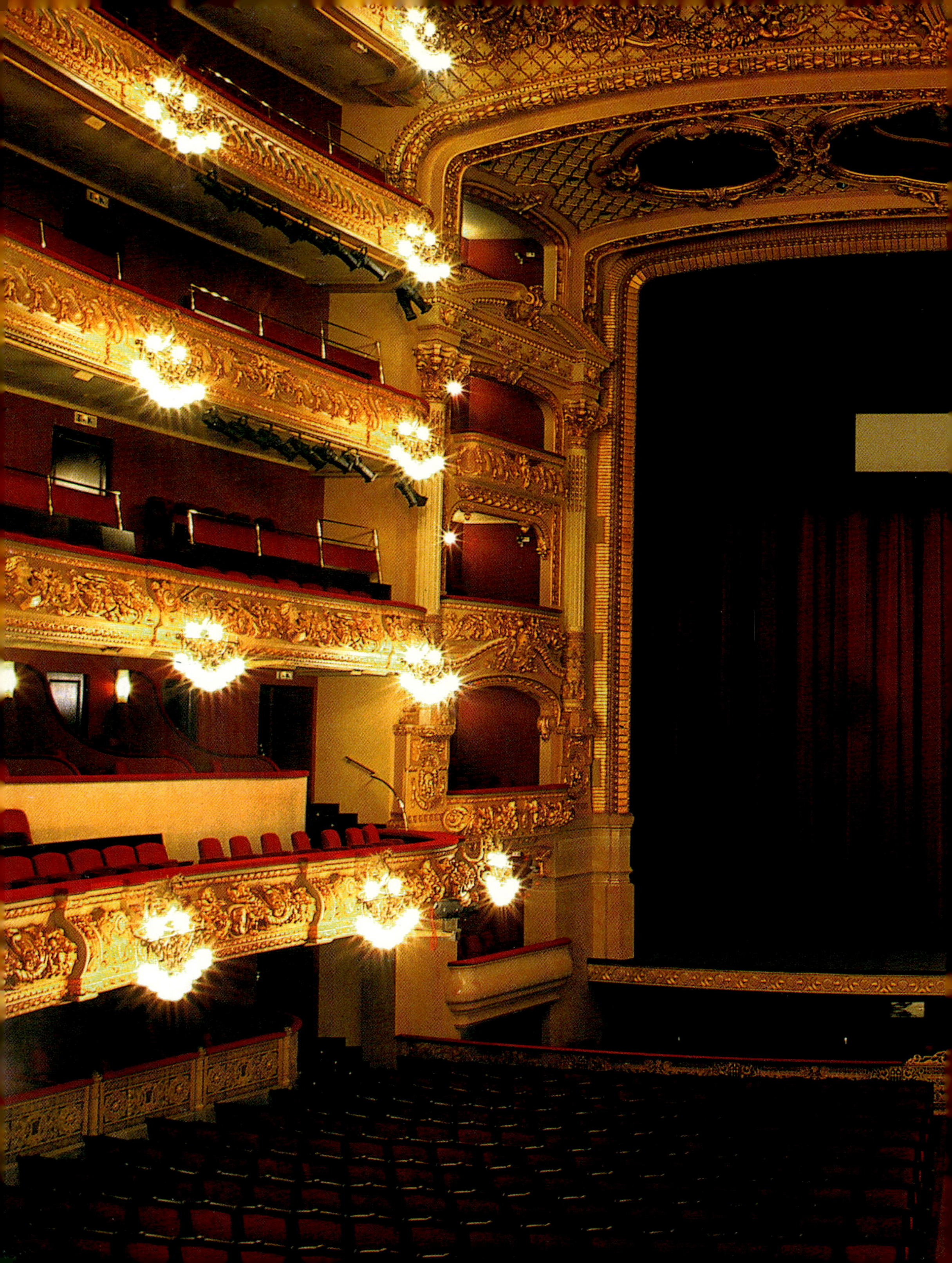

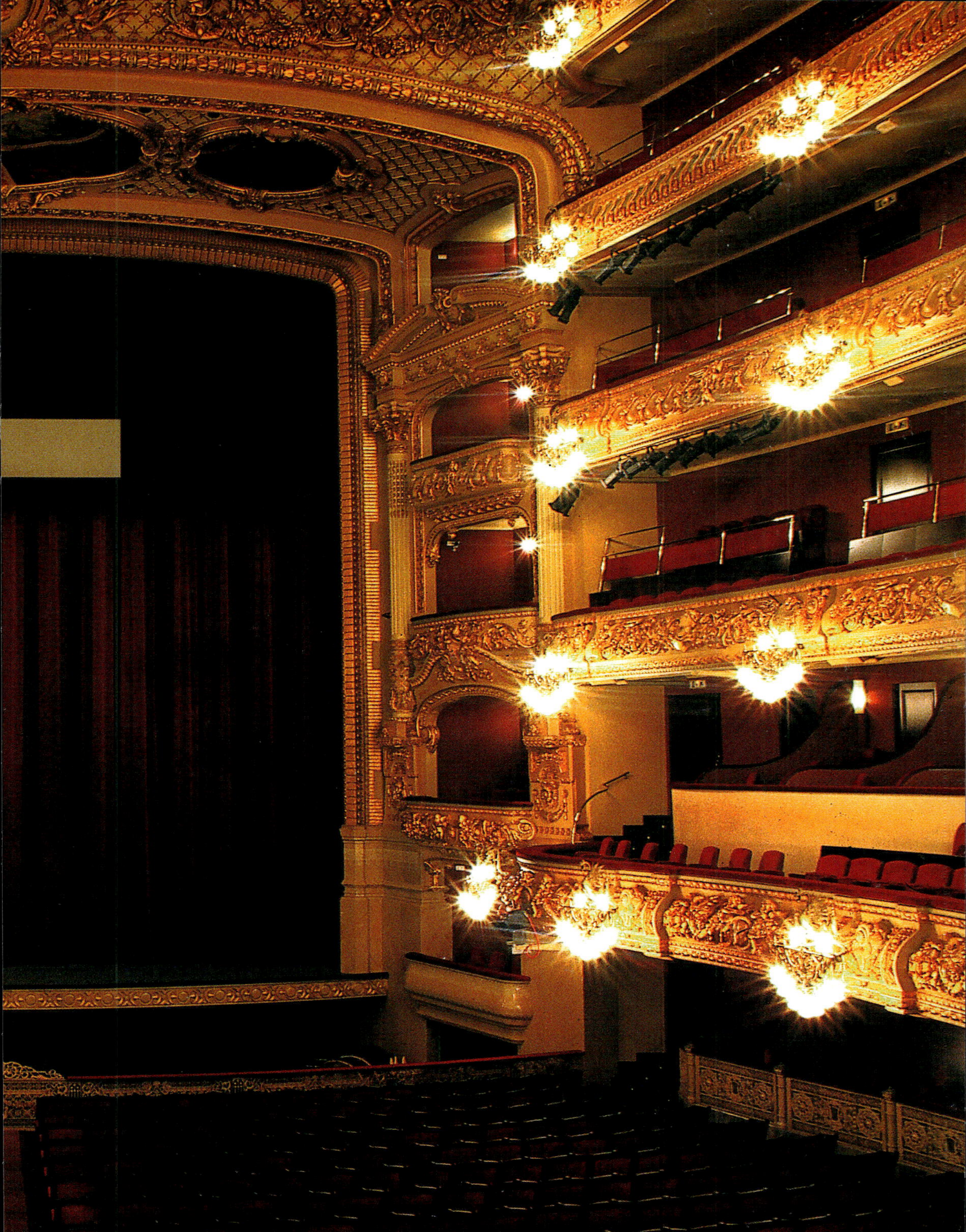

Howard Barker
Escenes d'una execució
Refugiats
Les Ballets de Monte-Carlo
Roméo et Juliette
Brian Friel
Translations

rimental theater in Barcelona is to be found in Artenbrut, Sala Becket, Espai Escènic Joan Brossa, Teatre Malic, Sala Muntaner, Teatre Nou Tantarantana, among others.

The world of the stage is, thus, well represented in the city, and this is partly true because there is a long tradition of Catalan artists in varied fields of interpretation. There is also the factor of the festivals referred to earlier, and all of these factors have made the city an inescapable reference point in this form of artistic expression.

The **cinema** also plays an important role in the life of Barcelonans. Recent years have seen the opening of numerous projection rooms. Whether because of the refurbishment projects of many old movie theaters or because of the creation of multicines in the new entertainment areas like the Maquinista, Barcelona Glòries, Maremàgnum, Diagonal Mar or Heron City, what is undeniable is that currently the city has more than 100 movie theaters. These are distributed through the city and although the large part offer dubbed versions, Barcelona also has a number of houses that offer films in the original version. They are spaces with a long movie tradition such as the Verdi, Renoir, Casablanca, Meliès or the Filmoteca de Catalunya. These places also program different cycles dedicated to directors, genres, producers, more alternative cinema, or old films. They thus represent new and important locales offering a new and interesting proposal for buffs of the seventh art.

Designed by the architect Ricardo Bofill, the Teatre Nacional de Catalunya (TNC), with a look between the traditional and the modern, has brought a new lease on life to a district that required a profound urban transformation. Similarly, the creation of the TNC has brought about the consolidation of an offer of high theatrical quality that optes for aesthetic risk, creativity, and the most innovative projects.

There are **other types of activities** that can be enjoyed at night, of course, such as trips to the Font Màgica de Montjuïc (the Magic Fountain), the work of the engineer Carles Buigas that mixes jets of water with a play of colored lights. It is a marvelous spectacle and not to be missed. Very close to these fountains, also on Montjuïc, is the Poble Espanyol (Spanish Village), constructed for the occasion of the 1929 Universal Exposition. The Village reproduces buildings and typical sights from all over Spain. Walking around the Poble Espanyol by day is a pleasure in itself because in addition to discovering many different architectural styles from Spain's different regions you can buy natural and handicraft products. But the complex remains open at night to offer concerts and other performances as well as numerous restaurants, nightclubs, bars and discos.

At the other end of the city, on Collserola Hill, is the only amusement park currently in operation in Barcelona. This is Tibidabo and, while the youngest members of your family will certainly enjoy a day trip more, from mid-afternoon till 1:00 in the morning, the summer closing time, you will be able to enjoy some very spectacular views of the city as well as all of the rides and attractions that stay open till closing time.

It is also true that in fair weather the number of nighttime activities increases, since people are apt to go out more and enjoy the street and combat the heat. This is the case with the Noches de la Pedrera (Nights at the Pedrera), where, during the summer months, there are visits to Gaudí's masterwork. The entrance ticket includes

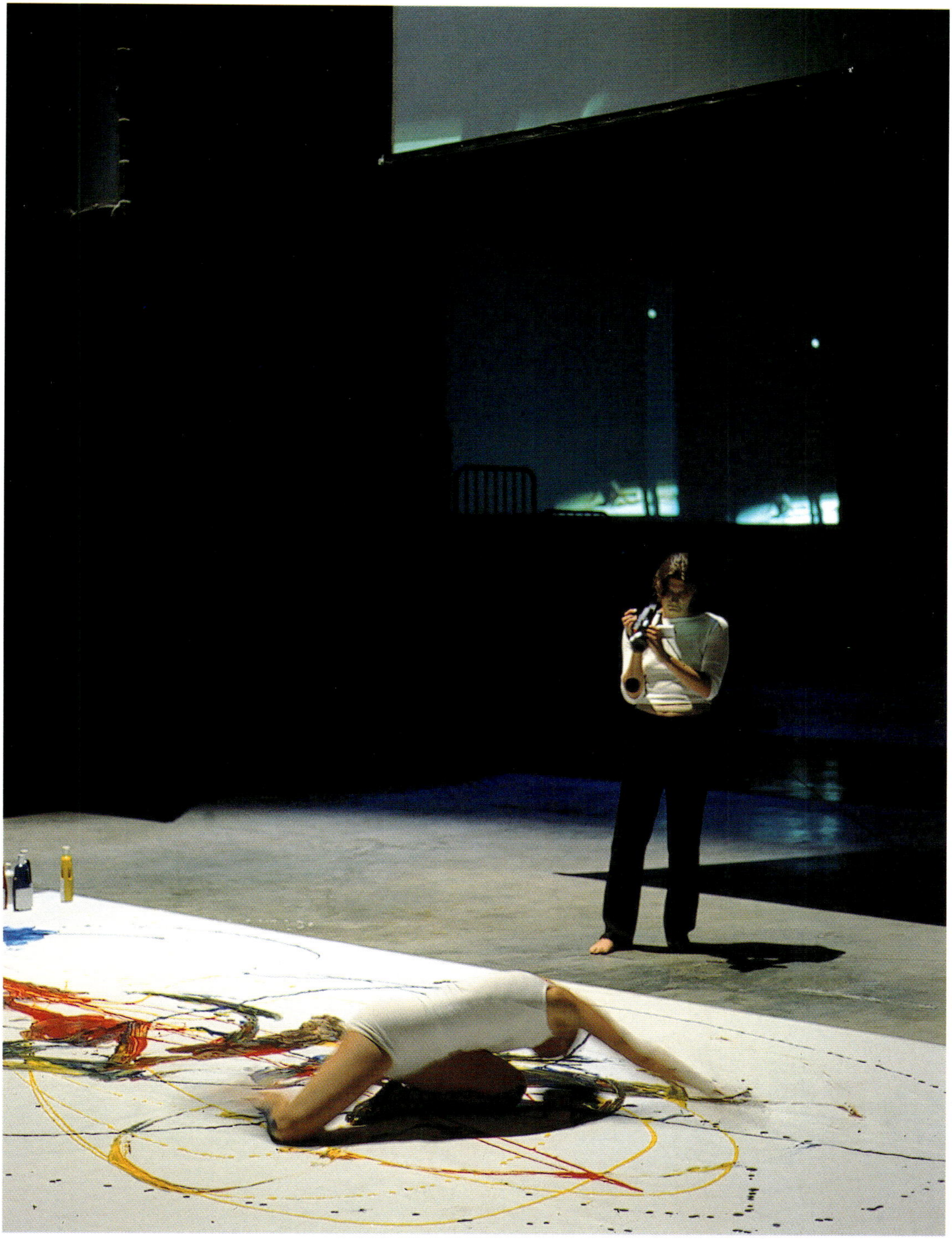

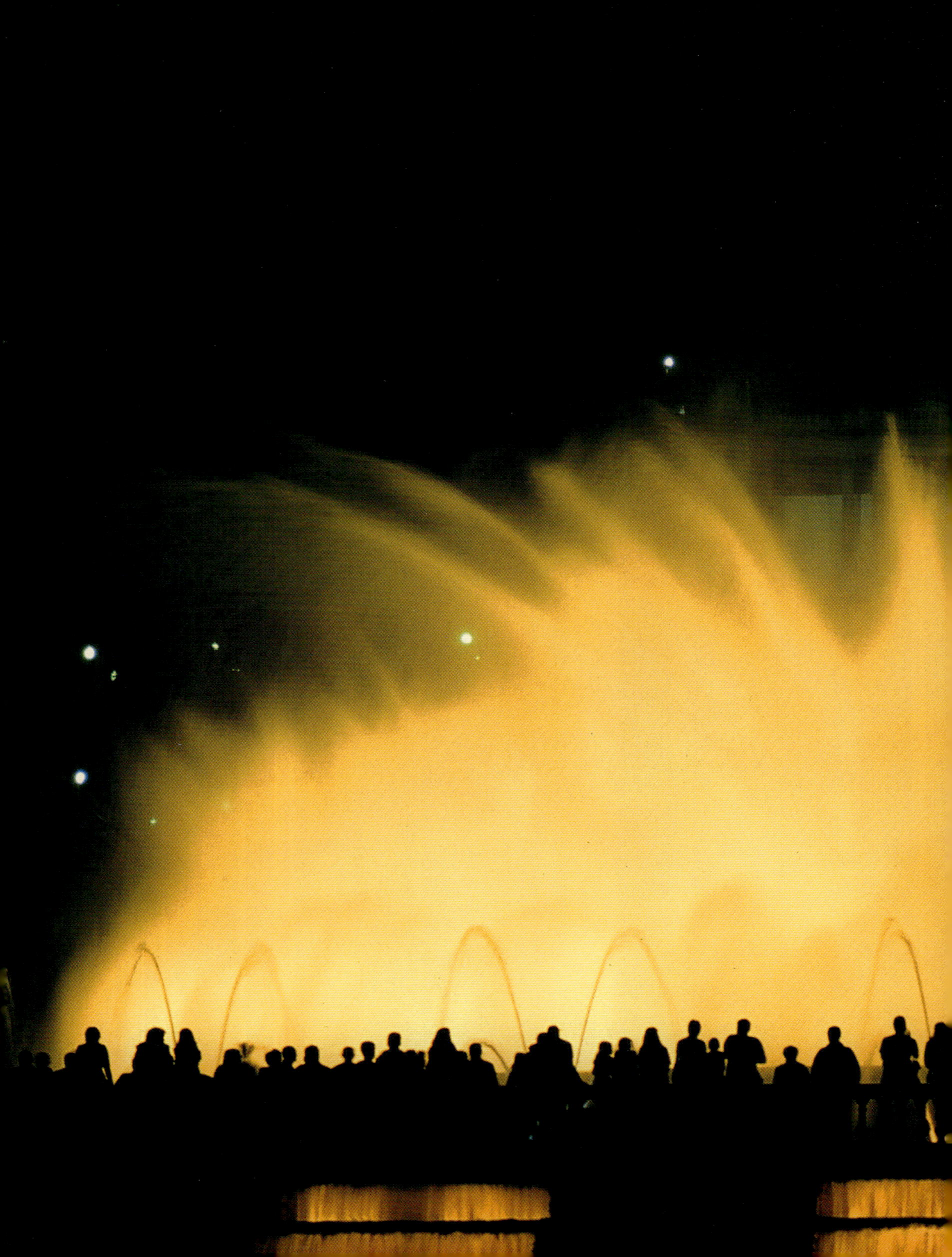

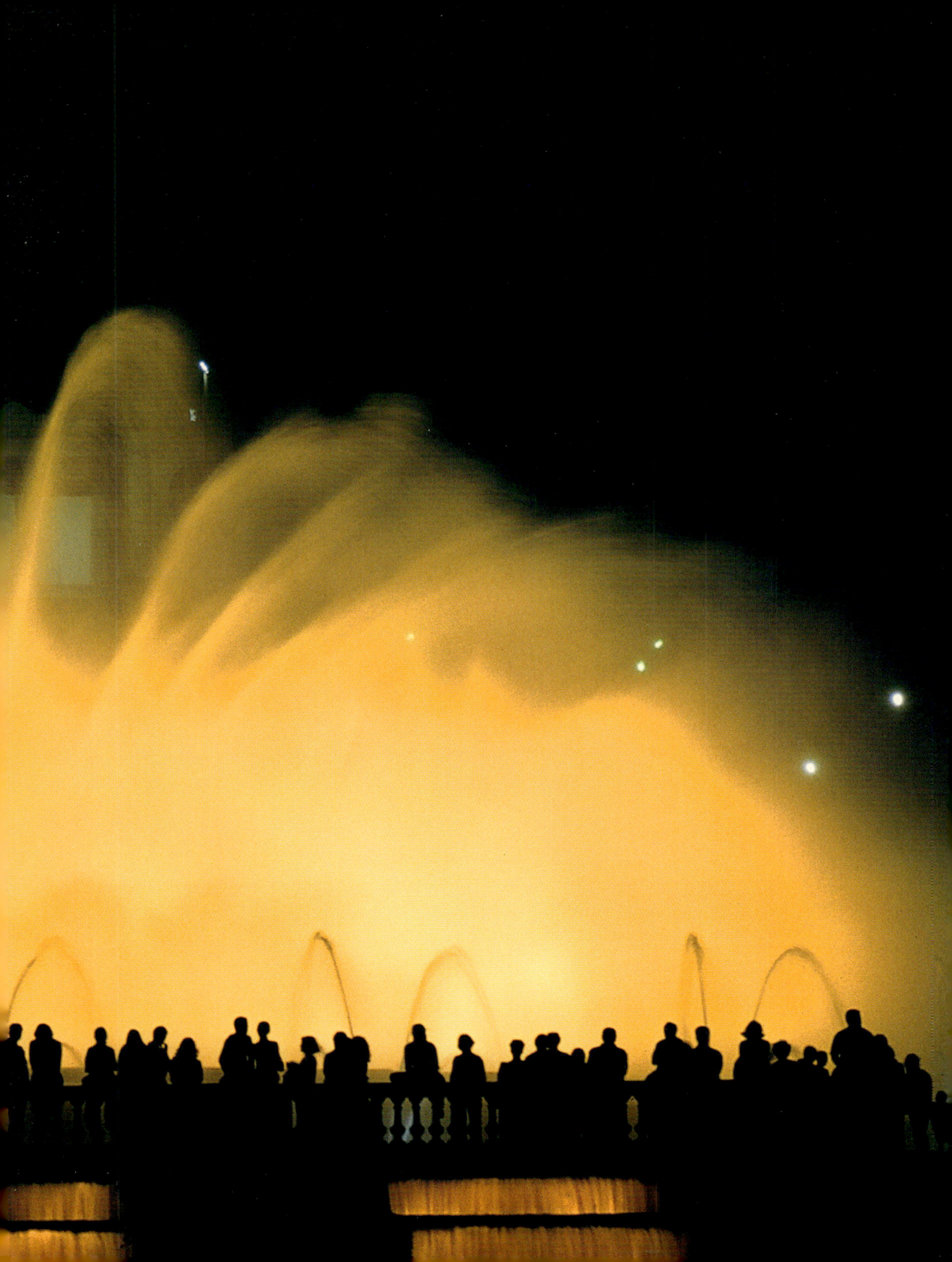

a drink and there are concerts programmed on the building's terraces, highly recommendable and unforgettable, especially if you are staying up late and want magnificent views. With the arrival of good weather, some of the city's parks program open-air concert cycles like those in Turó Parc.

While the majority of the museums close their doors at 21:00, some, like the art galleries, foundations, or centers, occasionally offer night shows. This is the case, for example, of the Museo de Cera (Wax Museum) which programs night visits. The entrance ticket to this singular museum also includes a complimentary drink.

There are other activities on offer from time to time during the night, such as fashion shows at the Pasarela Gaudí, some stores that stay open at night, or part of the night, at different times of the year, such as the handicrafts stands on the Gran Vía at Christmas and the Epiphany. These places, too, are well worth the visit.

Another proposal: visit the Gran Casino de Barcelona and try your luck at the games of chance. The current installations, inaugurated at the Port Olimpic in 1999, offer the possibility of dinner and music spectacles.

There are other shows for adults only that are also to be found in Barcelona, like the mythical Bagdad, on the Avinguda Paral.lel, the Merca-Show, Starlets or Mr.Dollar, to name only some of the locales that offer this type of entertainment. Barcelona is, as we have attempted to show, a city with an active and overflowing nightlife for all tastes.

constructed in 1929, on the event of the universal exposition in order to gather together in a single space the different architectural styles of spain, the poble espanyol shows itself to be one of the finest examples of spaces dedicated to the most emblematic and interesting art, entertainment, and culture in Barcelona, both by day and by night.

Finally, although there are certainly many activities left unmentioned, it should be remembered that Barcelona's cosmopolitan character has not made it forget its traditions. The city turns out en masse for its many fiestas and festivals, and at these times the nighttime activities take on even greater importance. In broad terms, we note simply that the **calendar of fiestas** begins, as in all other cities, on the night of the 31 of December to the 1 of January with the arrival of the New Year, a time when, once more, the party atmosphere extends into the early hours of the dawn. The Day of Dance (Día de la Danza), 29 April, includes a wide array of performances on many different stages and on the street. The April Fair (Feria de Abril), in spite of being an Andalusian tradition, is also celebrated in Catalonia and goes on, as the canons prescribe, until the wee hours with dancing to the rhythm of sevillanas, cante and wine.

With the coming of warmer weather, around the month of June, the Festival de Music Avanzada y Multimedia (Sónar) invades different spaces in the city. Also in June, and coinciding with the summer solstice, the fiesta of Sant Joan is celebrated, a markedly Mediterranean celebration with fireworks and which takes over the night in the city—all night long.

From June to August, Barcelona becomes a complete cultural capital. The Festival Grec arrives, an event organized by the City Council and bringing to different stages in the city the best in theater, dance, and music on a national and international level. Also during the festival months, numerous neighborhoods hold the fiestas dedicated to their patron saints, programming all sorts of events that go on until dawn. The most famous and popular of these take place in the neighborhoods of Gràcia and Sants.

The week of 24 September, Barcelona lives its largest fiesta, the Festas de la Mercè, the city's patron saint. Fireworks, concerts, correfocs (a fireworks procession with dragons)... and more, almost innumerable activities take place on these days when the hubbub fills the streets of the city center.

During the month of October the Festival de Jazz de Ciutat Vella and the Festival Internacional de Cine de Catalunya de Sitges are the main attractions (Sitges is a town very close to the city of Barcelona). Also in mid-October, the streets of the Ribera district fill up with music during the Ribermusic festival, and at the end of the month until December, jazz again takes over the city, this time in the guise of the Festival Internacional de Jazz de Barcelona. From the end of October till the beginning of November the Festival Internacional de Cine Gay y Lésbico (Lesbian and Gay International Film Festival). At the end of December and the beginning of January, it is again the turn of music, in this case at the Festival de Músicas Contemporáneas.

The salón gaudí is one of the most fascinating proposals for getting to know the latest trends in the fashion sector. New names in the field parade their work alongside the biggest names in catalan design.

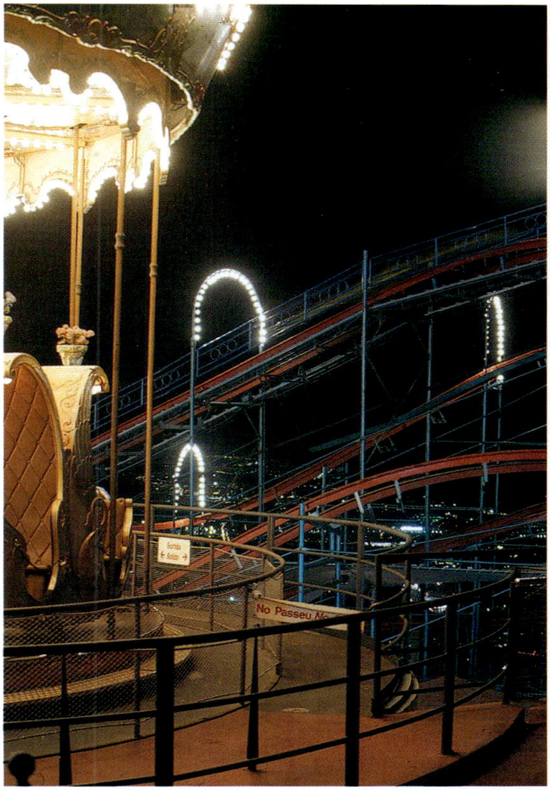

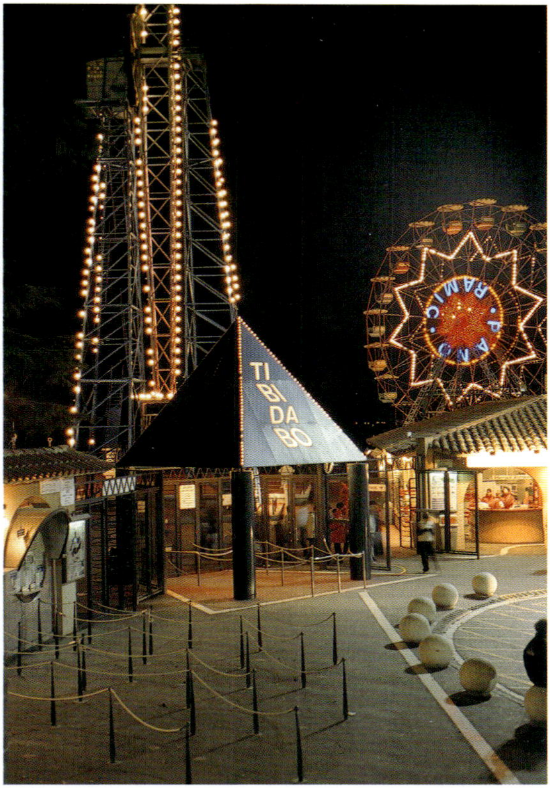
TI
BI
DA
BO

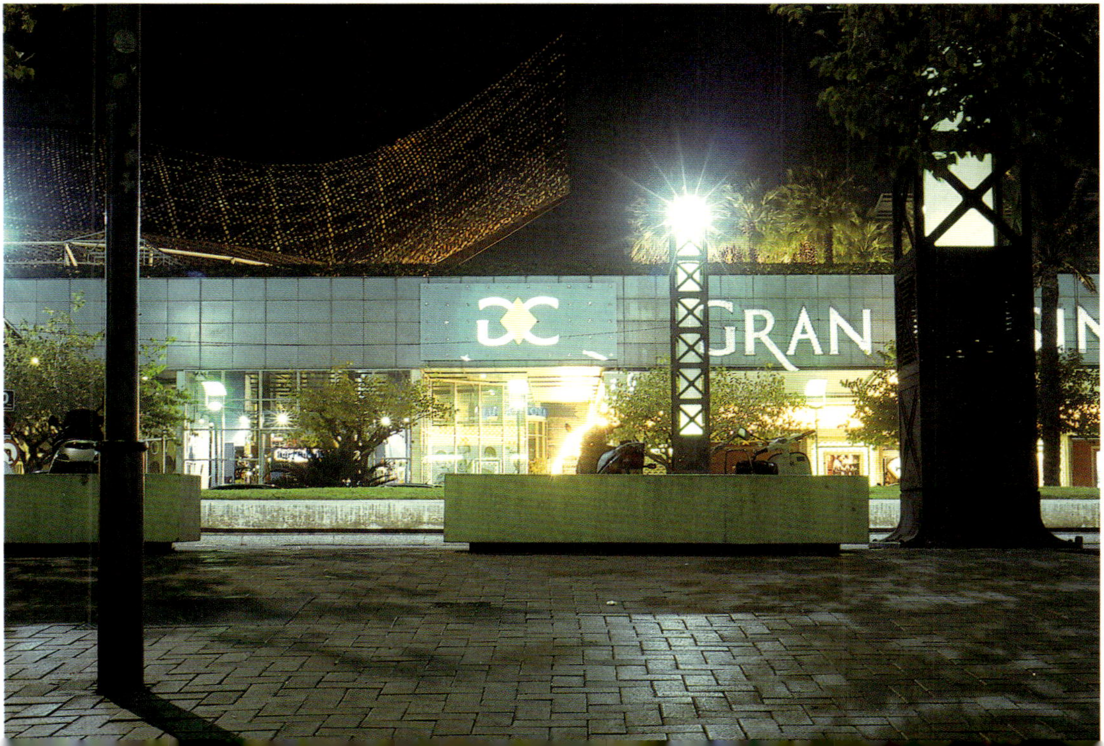
GRAN

Av. Rius i Taulet
Guardia Urbana
Mercat de les Flors
Teatre Grec
Font del Gat
Museus

Casa Ramona
Poble Espanyol
Palau Nacional
MNAC
Estadi Olímpic
Lluís Companys
Fira
5242 BGJ
4964 BBL

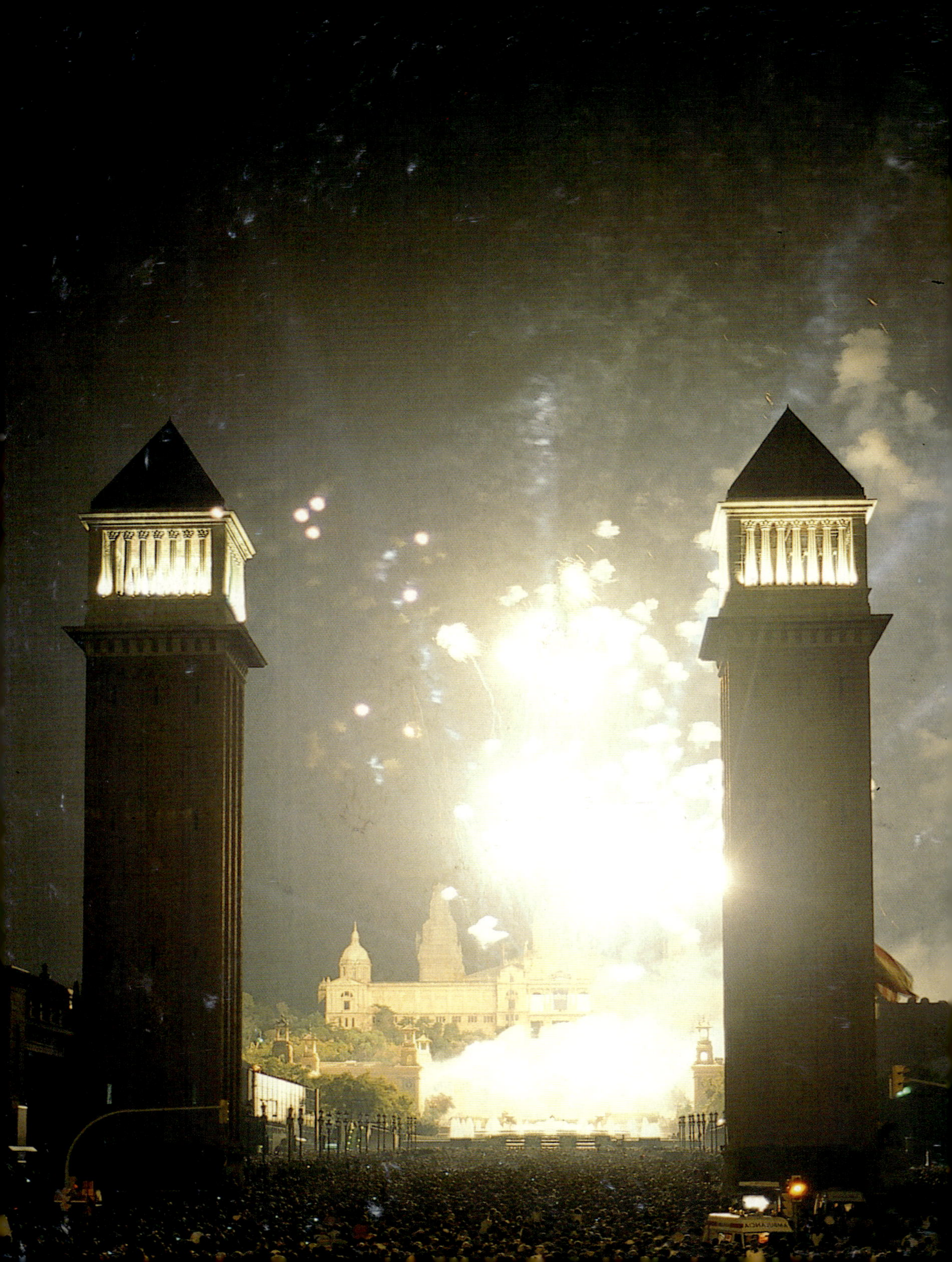

At the end of the Avinguda Maria Cristina, opposite the Palau Nacional, is the Font Màgica (Magic Fountain). The engineer Carles Buigas designed it on the occasion of the Universal Exposition of 1929 and the superb display of water, light, music, and color it offers is certainly worth seeing.

During the Mercè—the fiestas in honor of Barcelona's patron saint—numerous public spaces, like the cathedral or the plaça del Rei, become the improvised stages for different events on the city council's program. Music, fun, entertainment, and culture invade the streets and its inhabitants become the real protagonists of the night.

The CCCB (Centre de Culture Contemporània de Barcelona) is one of the artistic spaces that boast the greatest creativity and innovation in the city. The CCCB is a multidisciplinary institution which, in addition to organizing shows throughout the year, also programs all types of activities related to art, entertainment, and culture. An example of this may be seen in the European short films viewed annually in the open air during the month of September. The space is open to all new film languages, creativity, and experimentation.

Nighttime entertainment 115

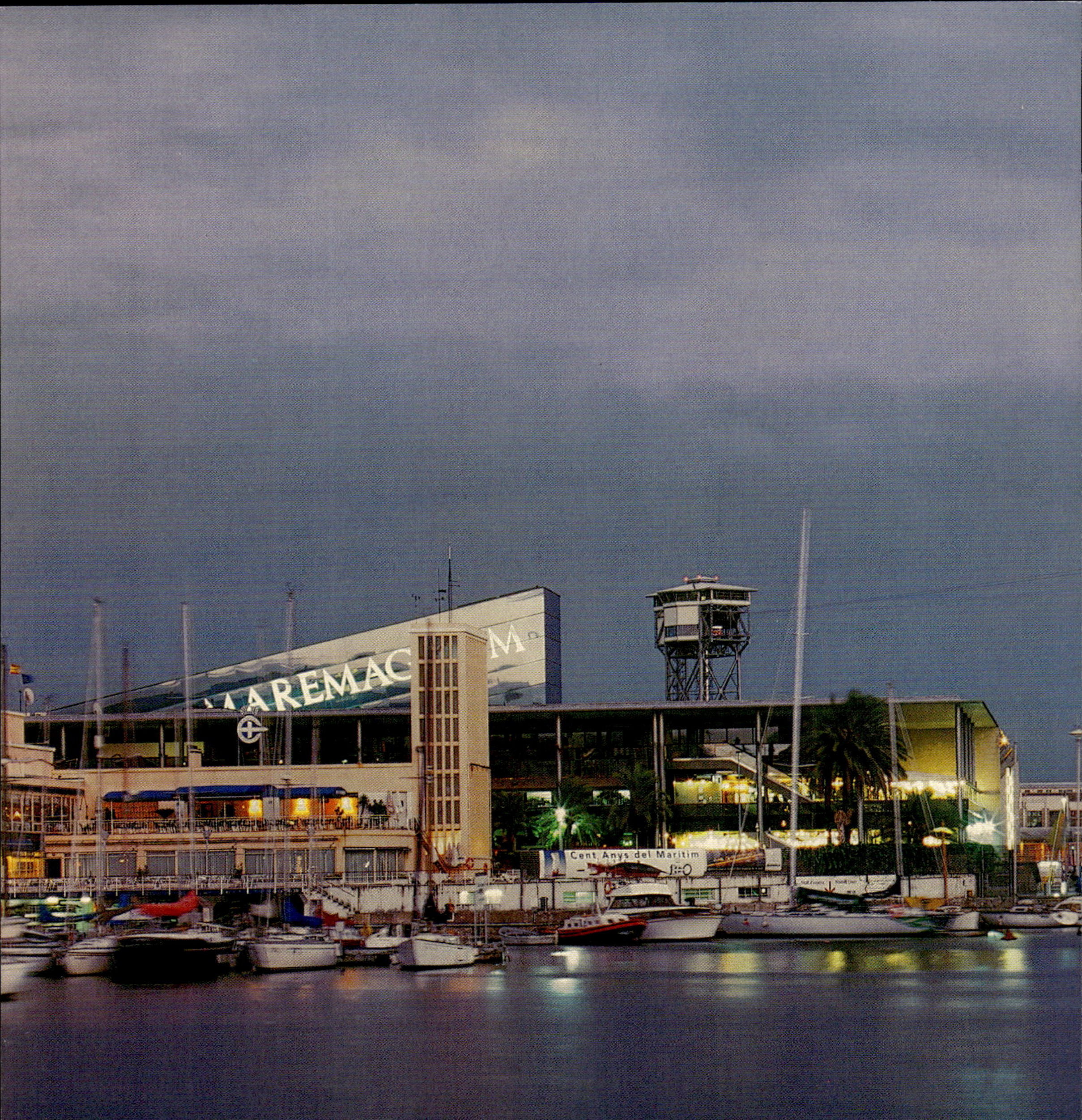
Cent Anys del Maritim

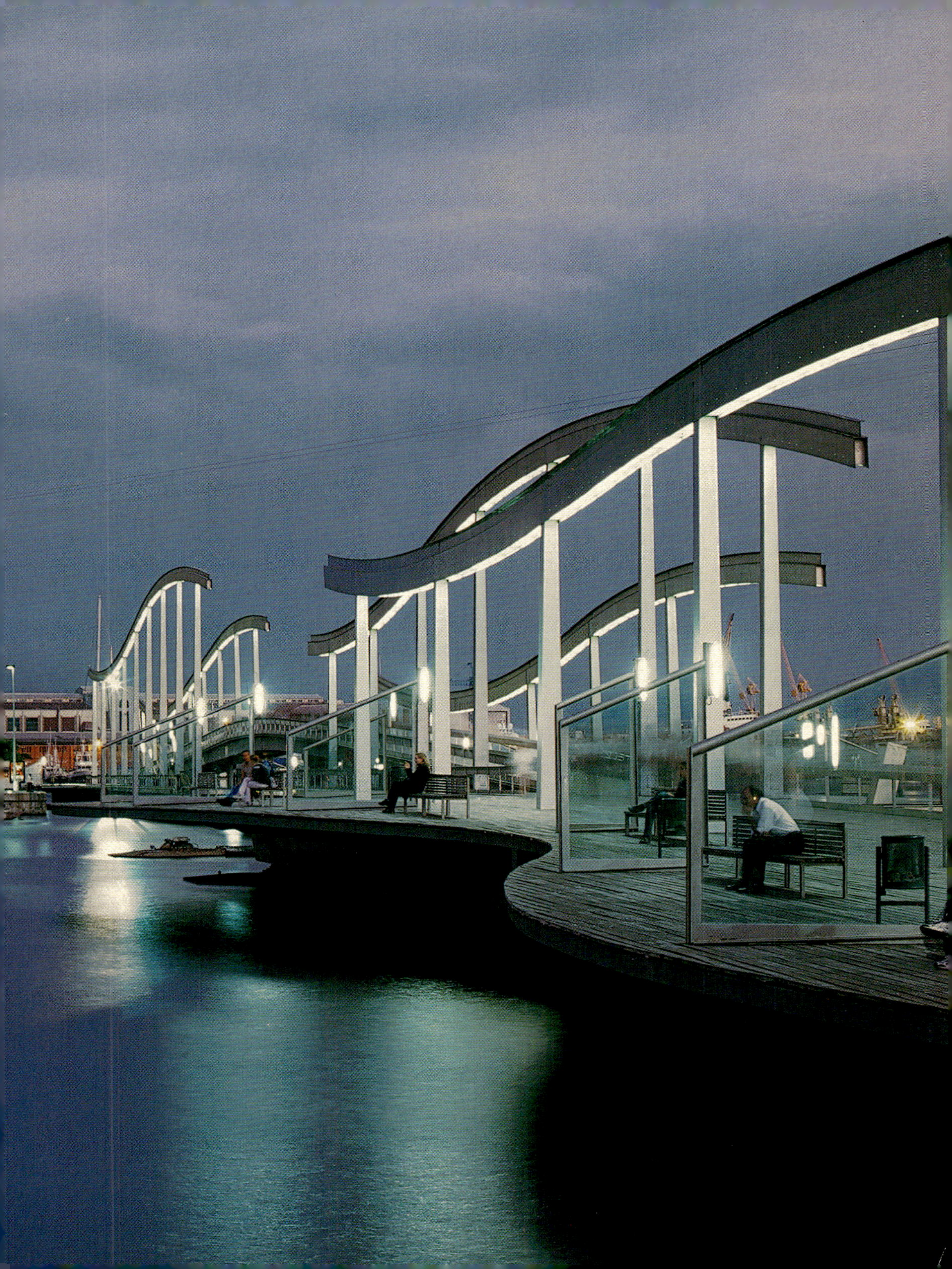

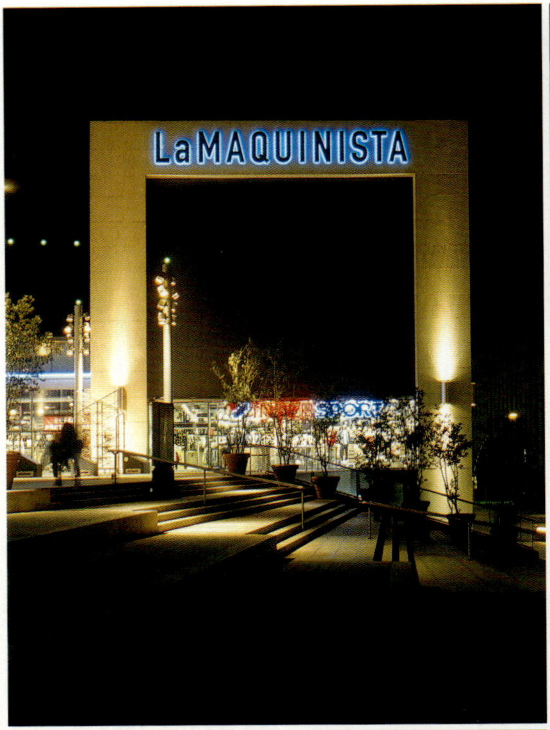
LaMAQUINISTA

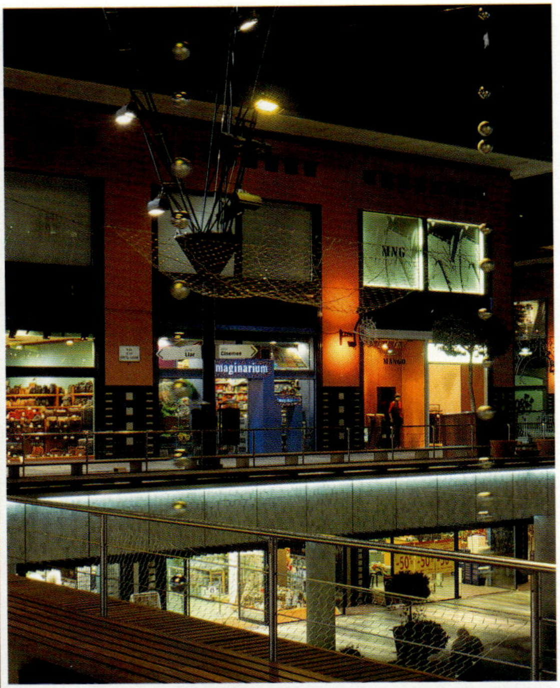
MNG

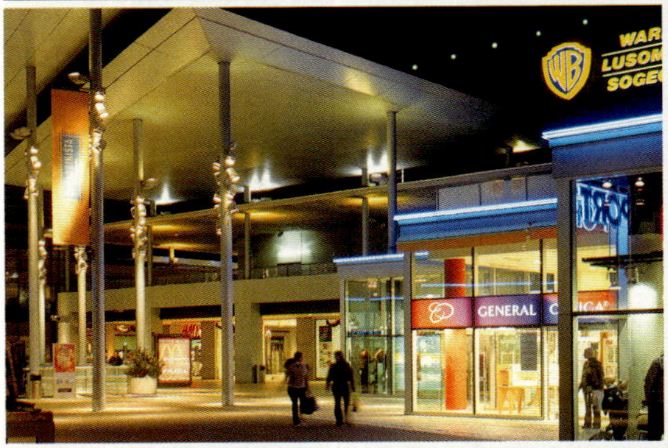
GENERAL

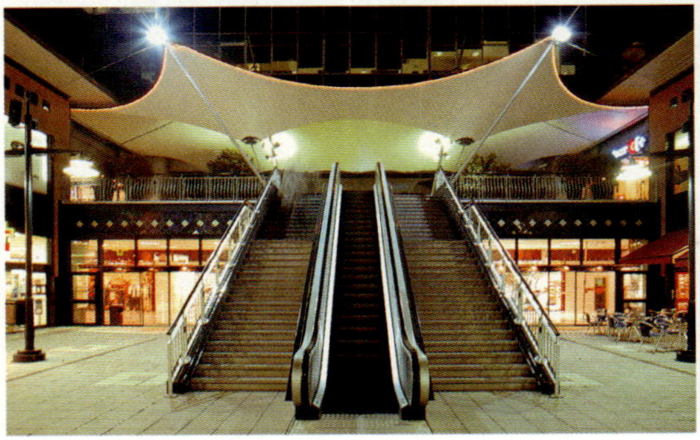

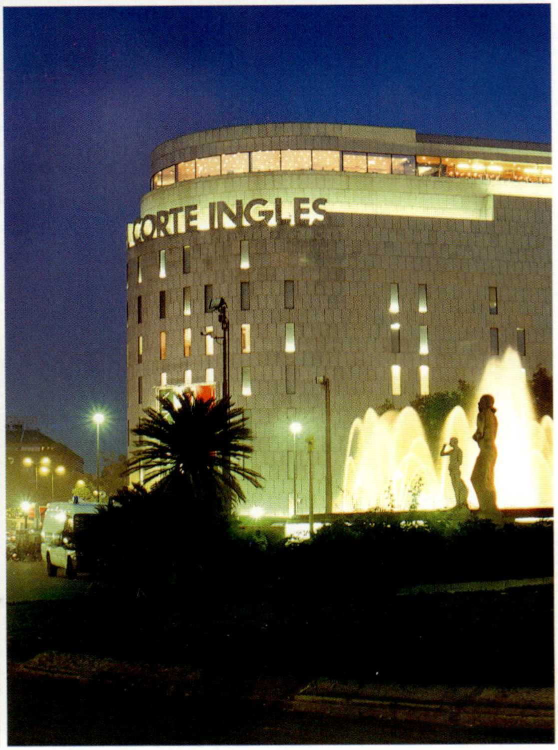
CORTE INGLES

nighttime entertainment 119

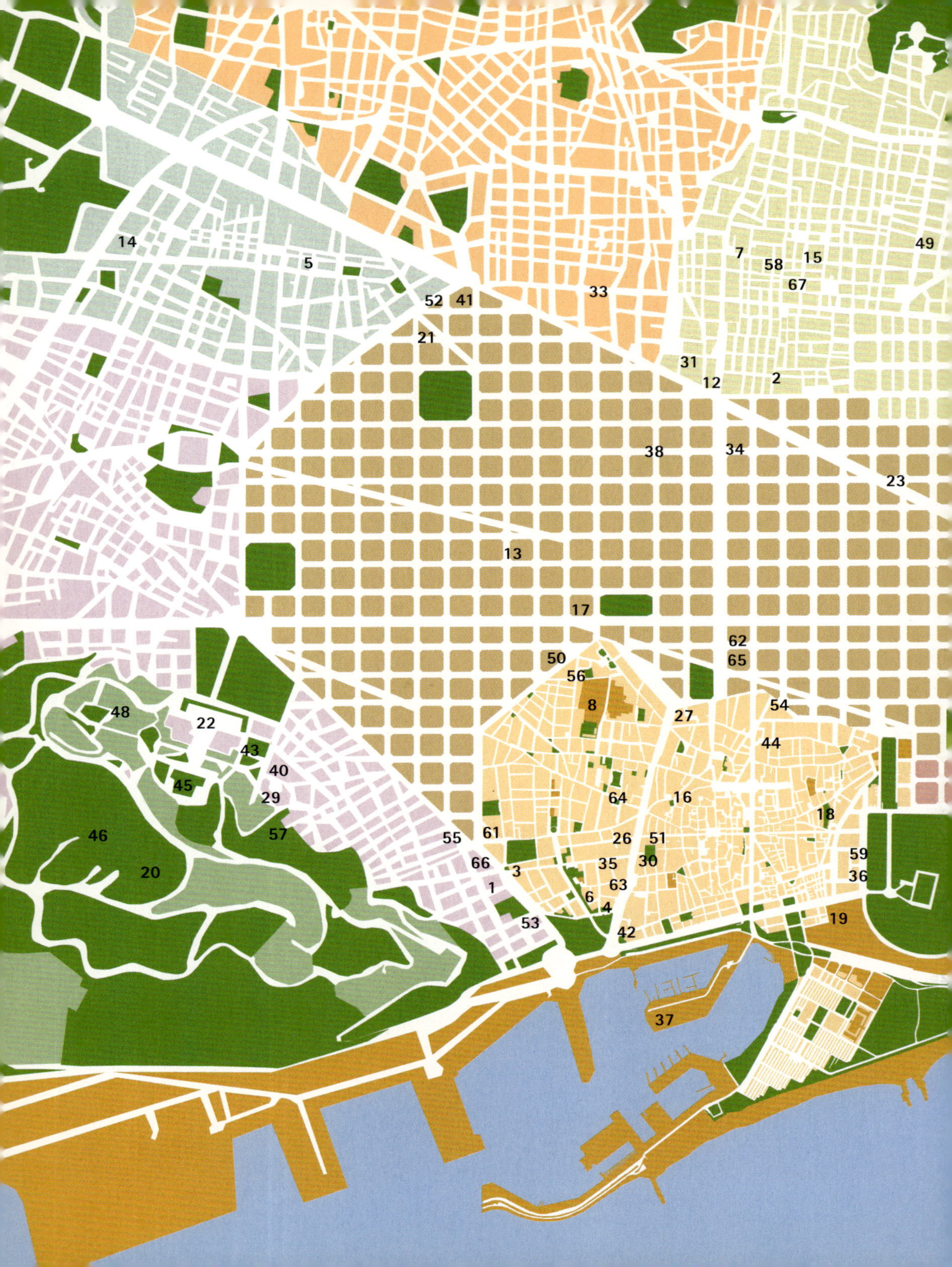
14
5
7
58
15
49
67
52
41
33
21
31
12
2
38
34
23
13
17
62
65
50
56
8
27
54
48
22
44
43
40
64
16
29
18
45
46
57
55
61
26
51
59
20
66
35
30
36
3
63
1
6
4
19
53
42
37

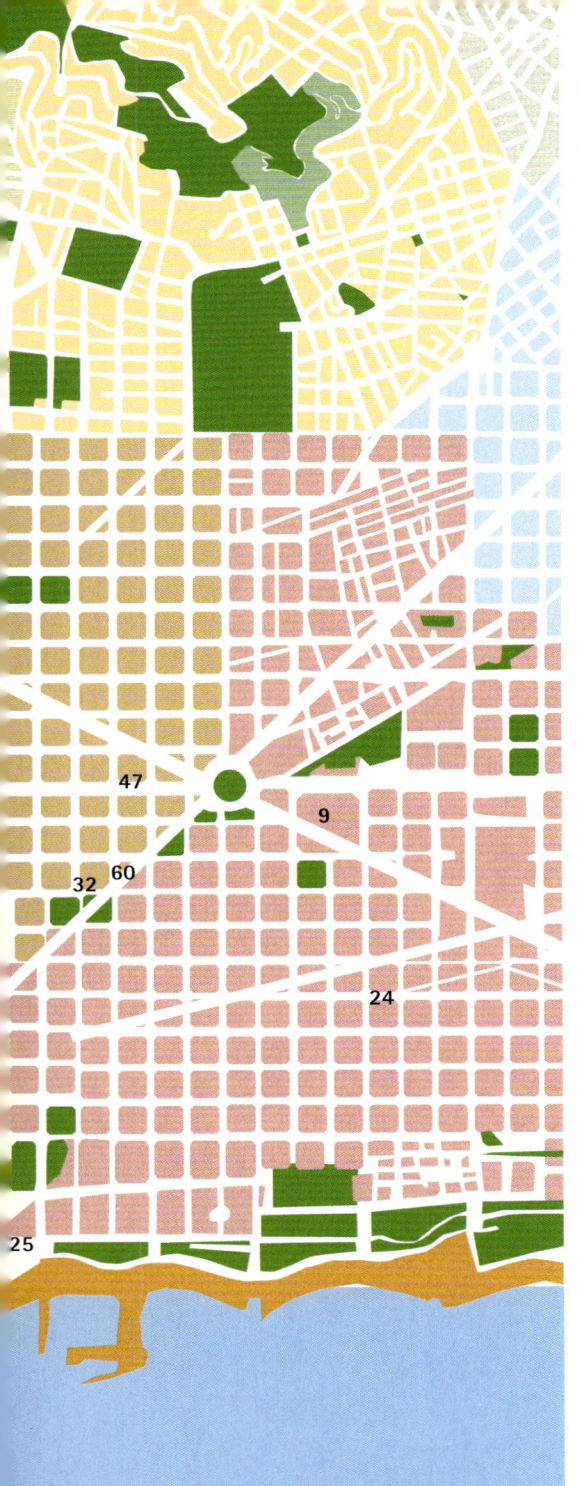

nighttime entertainment: practical information

1. APOLO. Nou de la Rambla, 113 ☎ 934 414 001
2. ARTENBRUT. Perill, 9-11 ☎ 934 579 705
3. BAGDAD. Nou de la Rambla, 103 ☎ 934 420 777
4. BAR PASTÍS. Santa Mònica, 4 ☎ 933 187 980
5. BIKINI. Déu i Mata, 105
6. CANGREJO. Montserrat, 9
7. CAT CENTRE ARTESÀ TRADICIONÀRIUS. Travessera de Sant Antoni, 6 ☎ 932 184 485
8. CENTRE DE CULTURA CONTEMPORÀNIA DE BARCELONA (CCCB). Montalegre, 5 ☎ 933 064 100
9. CENTRE COMERCIAL BARCELONA GLÒRIES. Avinguda Diagonal, 208 ☎ 934 860 511
10. CENTRE COMERCIAL DIAGONAL MAR. Avinguda Diagonal, 35 (not on map)
11. CENTRE COMERCIAL LA MAQUINISTA. Passeig Potosí, 2 ☎ 902 233 343 (not on map)
12. CINEMA CASABLANCA. Passeig de Gràcia, 115 ☎ 932 184 345
13. CINEMA MELIÈS. Villarroel, 102 ☎ 934 510 051
14. CINEMA RENOIR. Eugeni d'Ors, 12 ☎ 934 905 510
15. CINEMES VERDI. Verdi, 32 ☎ 932 387 990
16. CÍRCOL MALDÀ. Pi, 5 ☎ 934 124 386
17. DOMÈSTIC. Diputació, 215 ☎ 934 531 661
18. ESPAI ESCÈNIC JOAN BROSSA. Allada Vermell, 13 ☎ 933 101 364
19. ESTACIÓ DE FRANÇA. Avinguda Marquès d'Argentera, 6
20. ESTADI OLÍMPIC. Passeig Olímpic, 17-19 ☎ 934 262 089
21. FILMOTECA DE CATALUNYA. Avinguda Sarrià, 33 ☎ 934 107 590
22. FONT MÀGICA. Plaça Carles Buïgas
23. FUNDACIÓ LA CAIXA. Passeig Sant Joan, 102 ☎ 934 768 600

24. GARATGE. Pallars, 195 ☎ 933 091 438
25. GRAN CASINO BARCELONA. Marina, 19-21 ☎ 932 257 878
26. GRAN TEATRE DEL LICEU. Rambla, 51-59 ☎ 934 859 913
27. HARD ROCK CAFÉ. Plaça Catalunya, 21 ☎ 932 702 305
28. HERON CITY. Passatge Andreu Nin, s/n ☎ 902 333 231 (not on map)
29. INSTITUT DEL TEATRE. Plaça Margarida Xirgu, 1 ☎ 932 273 900
30. JAMBOREE. Plaça Reial, 17 ☎ 933 017 564
31. JOVE TEATRE REGINA. Sèneca, 22 ☎ 932 181 512
32. AUDITORI. Lepant, 150 ☎ 933 171 096/932 479 300
33. L'ESPAI. Travessera de Gràcia, 63 ☎ 934 143 133
34. LA PEDRERA. Passeig de Gràcia, 92
35. LONDON BAR. Nou de la Rambla, 34 ☎ 933 185 261
36. MAGIC. Passeig Picasso, 40 ☎ 933 107 267
37. MAREMÀGNUM. Moll d'Espanya, s/n ☎ 902 333 231
38. MEDITERRÁNEO. Balmes, 129
39. MERCA-SHOW. Avinguda Principal, s/n, Mercabarna (Zona Franca) ☎ 932 630 091 (not on map)
40. MERCAT DE LES FLORS. Lleida, 59 ☎ 934 261 875
41. MR. DOLLAR. Avinguda Josep Tarradellas, 140 ☎ 934 391 815
42. MUSEU DE CERA. Passatge Banca, 5 ☎ 933 172 649/933 025 167
43. PALAU D'ESPORTS. Joaquim Blume, s/n ☎ 934 232 089
44. PALAU DE LA MÚSICA CATALANA. Sant Francesc de Paula, 2 ☎ 932 681 000
45. PALAU NACIONAL. Parc de Montjuïc ☎ 936 220 376/375

46. PALAU SANT JORDI. Passeig Olímpic, 5-7 ☎ 934 262 089
47. PLAZA DE TOROS MONUMENTAL. Gran Via, 747 ☎ 932 455 802
48. POBLE ESPANYOL. Avinguda Marquès de Comillas, 25 ☎ 933 257 866
49. SALA BECKET. Ca l'Alegre de Dalt, 55 bis ☎ 932 845 312
50. SALA MUNTANER. Muntaner, 4 ☎ 934 515 752
51. SIDECAR. Heures, 4-6 ☎ 933 021 586
52. STARLETS. Avinguda Sarrià, 44 ☎ 934 309 156
53. TEATRE APOLO. Avinguda Paral·lel, 57 ☎ 934 419 007
54. TEATRE BORRÀS. Plaça Urquinaona, 9 ☎ 934 121 582
55. TEATRE CONDAL. Avinguda Paral·lel, 91 ☎ 934 423 132/934 428 584
56. TEATRE GOYA. Joaquín Costa, 68 ☎ 933 181 984
57. TEATRE GREC. Passeig Santa Madrona, 36 ☎ 933 017 775
58. TEATRE LLIURE. Montseny, 47 ☎ 932 189 251
59. TEATRE MALIC. Fusina, 3 ☎ 933 107 035
60. TEATRE NACIONAL DE CATALUNYA. Plaça de les Arts, 1 ☎ 933 065 700/706
61. TEATRE NOU TANTARANTANA. Flors, 22 ☎ 934 417 022
62. TEATRE NOVEDADES. Casp, 1 ☎ 934 121 175
63. TEATRE PRINCIPAL. Rambla, 27 ☎ 933 014 750
64. TEATRE ROMEA. Hospital, 51 ☎ 933 015 504
65. TEATRE TÍVOLI. Casp, 8 ☎ 934 122 063
66. TEATRE VICTÒRIA. Avinguda Paral·lel, 67 ☎ 934 432 929
67. TEATRENEU. Terol, 26 ☎ 932 857 900
68. TIBIDABO. Plaça Tibidabo, 3 ☎ 932 117 942 (not on map)

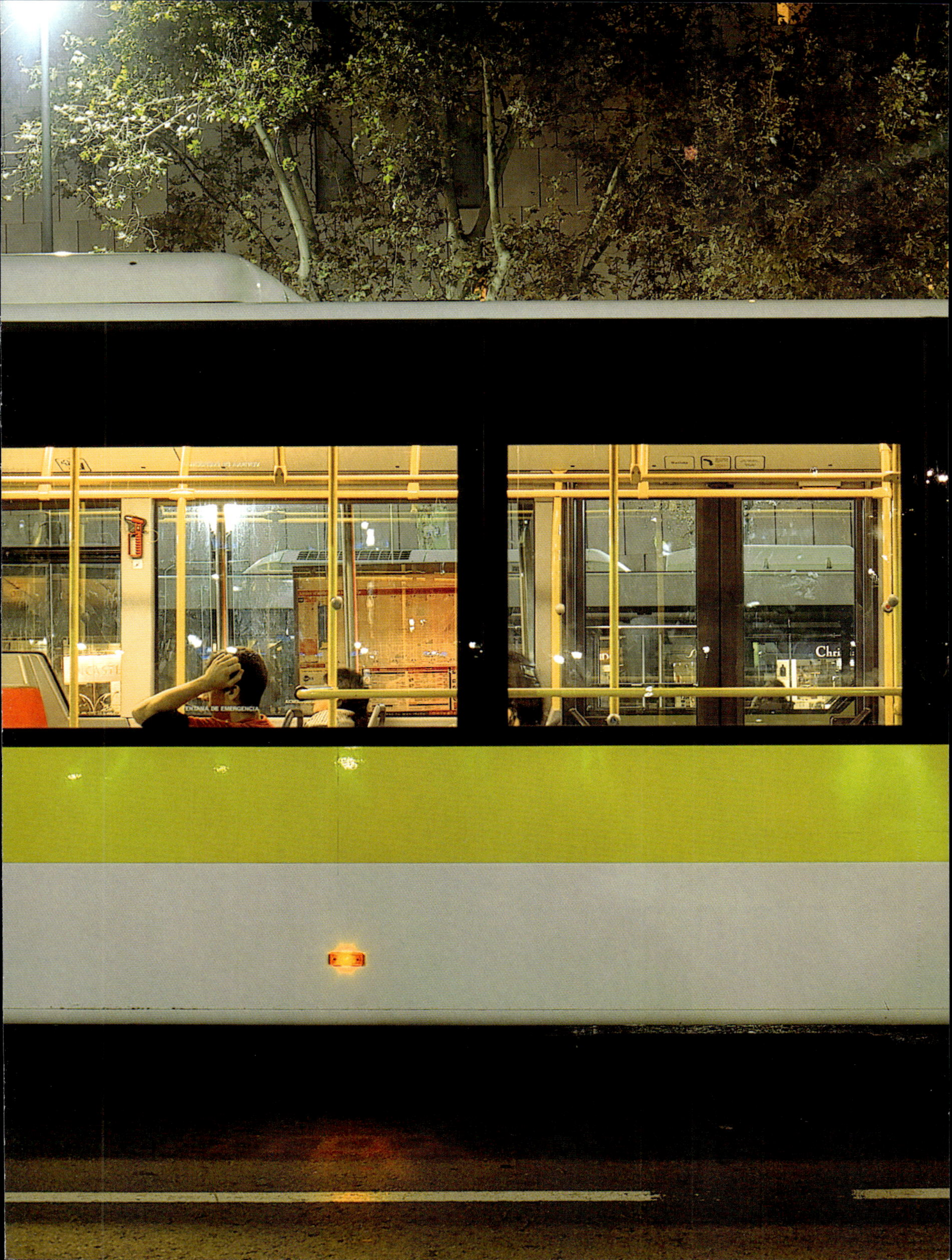

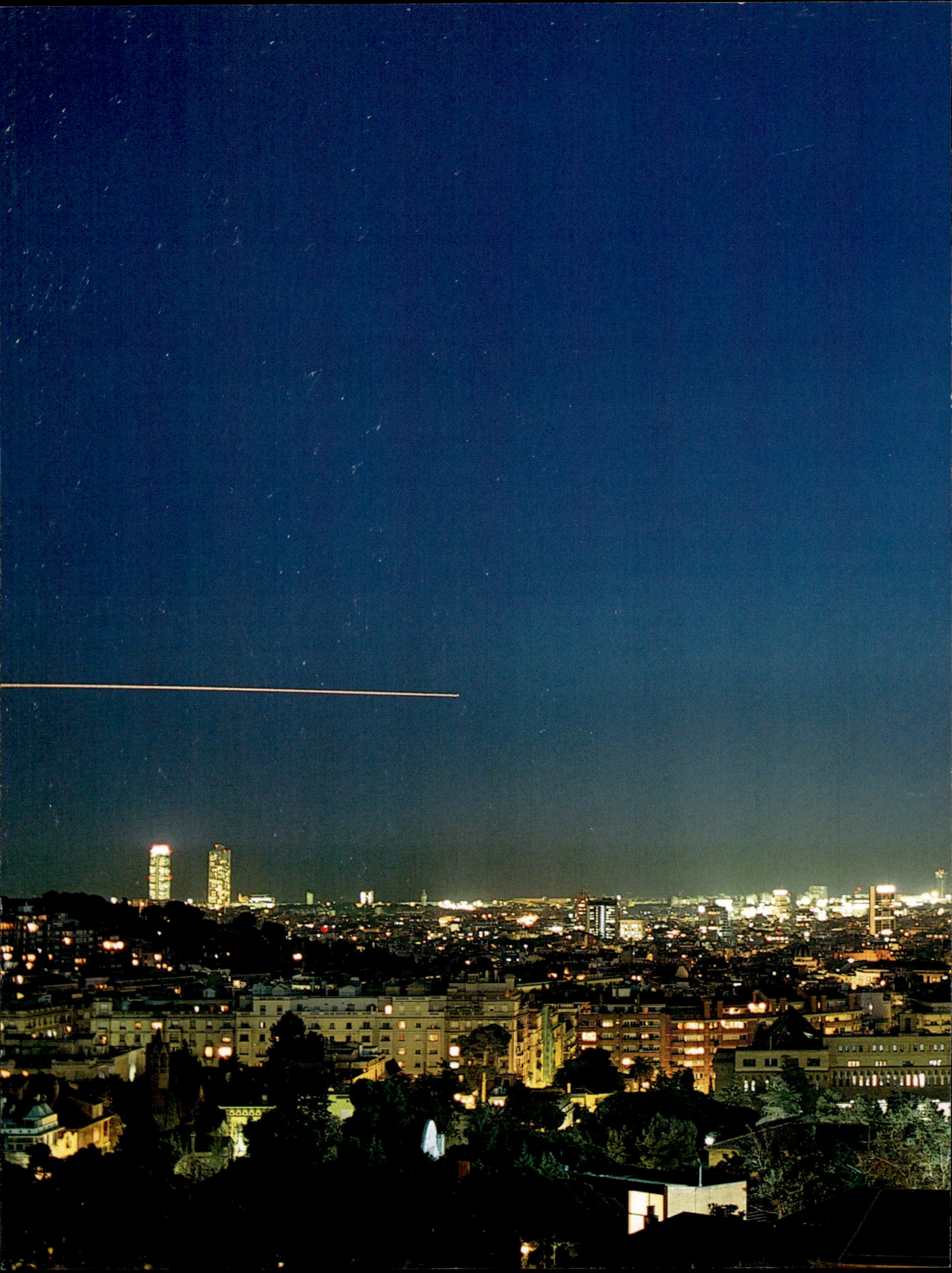

Other titles by

FUNDICIÓN, 15 Polígono Industrial Santa Ana 28529 Rivas-Vaciamadrid Madrid Tel. 34 91 666 50 01 Fax 34 91 301 26 83 asppan@asppan.com www.onlybook.com

The Best of Lofts
ISBN (E/GB): 95-09575-84-4

The Best of Bars & Restaurants
ISBN (E/GB): 95-09575-86-0

The Best of American Houses
ISBN (E/GB): 98-79778-17-0

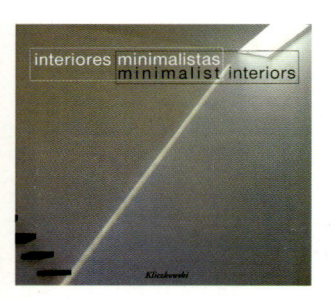

Interiores minimalistas/Minimalist Interiors
ISBN (E/GB): 98-79778-16-2

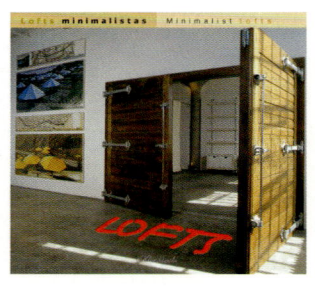

Lofts minimalistas/Minimalist lofts
ISBN (E/GB): 84-89439-55-9

Estancias Argentinas
ISBN (E/GB): 987-97781-9-7

Guggenheim
ISBN (E): 84-89439-52-4
ISBN (GB): 84-89439-53-2
ISBN (D): 84-89439-54-0
ISBN (P): 84-89439-63-X

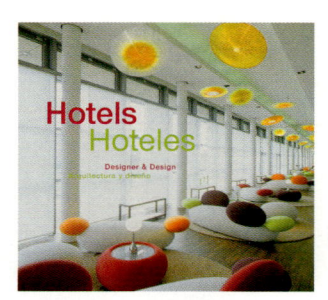

Hotels. Designer & Design
Hoteles. Arquitectura y Diseño
ISBN (E/GB): 84-89439-61-3

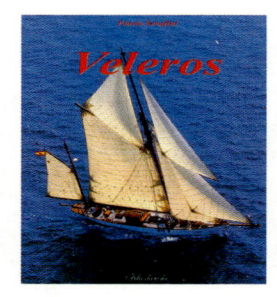

Veleros de época
ISBN (E): 987-9474-06-6

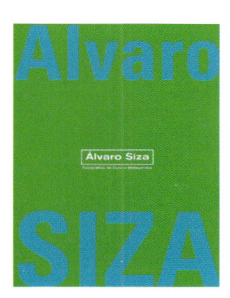

Álvaro Siza
ISBN: (E) 84-89439-70-2
ISBN: (P) 972-576-220-7

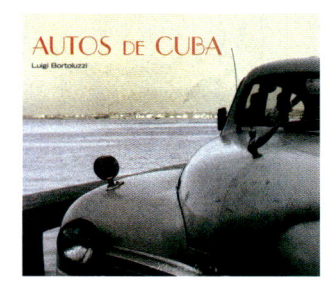

Autos de Cuba
ISBN: (E) 84-89439-62-1

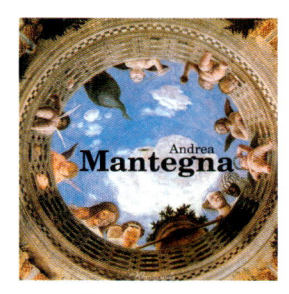

Andrea Mantegna
ISBN: (E) 987-9474-10-4

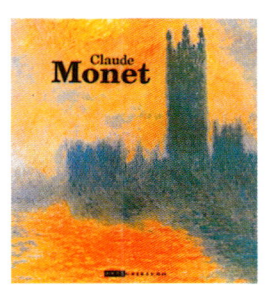

Claude Monet
ISBN: (E) 987-9474-03-1

Rembrandt
ISBN: (E) 987-9474-09-0

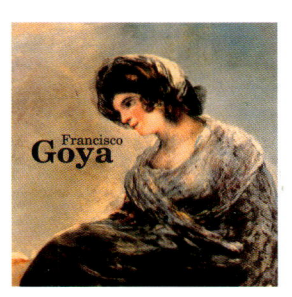

Francisco Goya
ISBN: (E) 987-9474-11-2

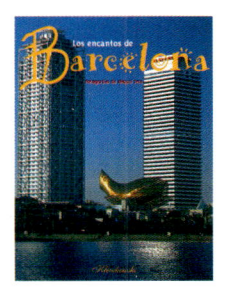

Los encantos de Barcelona/
Barcelona Style
ISBN (E): 84-89439-56-7
ISBN (GB): 84-89439-57-5

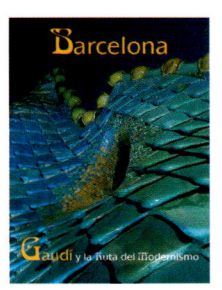

Barcelona, Gaudí y la ruta del Modernismo/
Barcelona, Gaudí and Modernism
ISBN: (E)   84-89439-50-8
ISBN: (GB) 84-89439-51-6
ISBN: (D)   84-89439-58-3
ISBN: (IT)   84-89439-59-1
ISBN: (JP)   84-89439-60-5

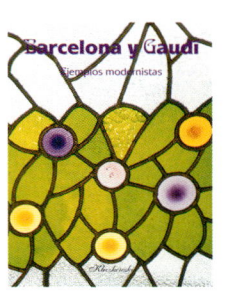

Barcelona y Gaudí. Ejemplos
modernistas/Barcelona and Gaudí.
Examples of Modernist architecture
ISBN: (E)   84-89439-64-8
ISBN: (GB) 84-89439-65-6

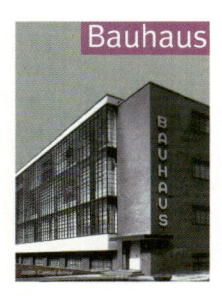

Bauhaus
ISBN (E): 98-79778-14-6

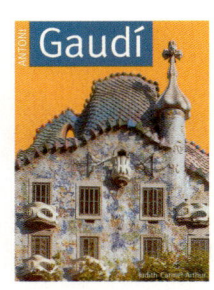

Antoni Gaudí
ISBN (E): 98-75130-09-5

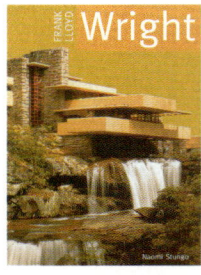

Frank Lloyd Wright
ISBN (E): 98-79778-11-1

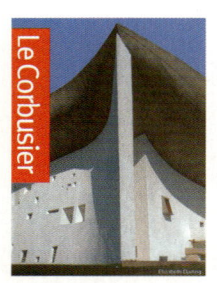

Le Corbusier
ISBN (E): 98-79778-13-8

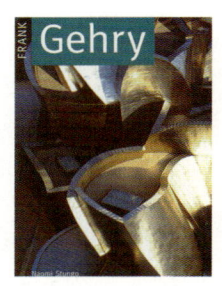

Frank Gehry
ISBN (E):   85868-879-5
ISBN (GB): 1-85868-879-5

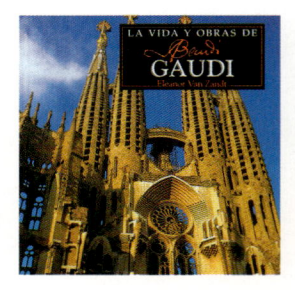

La vida y obras de Antoni Gaudí
ISBN (E): 950-9575-78-X

Cafés. Designer & Design
Cafés. Arquitectura y Diseño
ISBN (E/GB): 84-89439-69-9

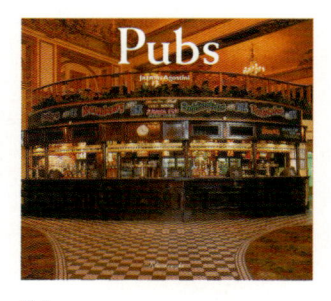

Pubs
ISBN: (E) 84-89439-68-0

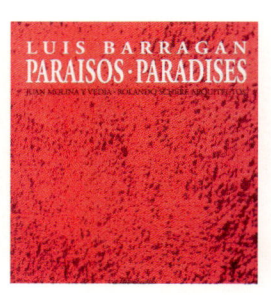

Luis Barragán
ISBN: (E/GB) 987-9474-02-3